The Elegant Shed

The Eleg

New Zealand Arc

ant Shed

ecture since 1945

David Mitchell
and
Gillian Chaplin

Auckland
Oxford University Press
Melbourne Oxford New York

Oxford University Press

Oxford London Glasgow New York Toronto
Delhi Bombay Calcutta Madras Karachi
Kuala Lumpur Singapore Hong Kong Tokyo
Nairobi Dar es Salaam Cape Town
Melbourne Auckland
and associates in
Beirut Berlin Ibadan Mexico City Nicosia

First published 1984
© David Mitchell and Gillian Chaplin 1984

ISBN 0 19 558125 3

Designed by Ross Ritchie
Photoset in Palatino and printed by Whitcoulls Ltd, Christchurch
Published by Oxford University Press
5 Ramsgate Street, Auckland, New Zealand

Contents

Acknowledgements

The television series 'The Elegant Shed' was screened while this book was being written and photographed. The six television episodes almost match the six chapters of the book, at least in structure and subject. But the book is not frozen television: to withstand the terrible scrutiny of the reader the words have had to be rewritten, the pictures retaken. We are grateful to Television New Zealand and the people of Kaleidoscope for the opportunity to do the groundwork of this book, and to Jennifer Lee-Lewes, whose research for the television series we used in the book.

Our greatest thanks are due to Wendy Garvey, Librarian at the University of Auckland School of Architecture, for her ceaseless supply of unique files, rare photographs, patience and humour. Whenever she could, she has supported David's pronouncements with an underpinning of hard fact. We are grateful for the help given by Sarah Treadwell, Nick Stanish, Kerry Morrow, Mike Austin, Allan Wild, the Jackson family, Alexa Johnston, John Nicol, Miles Warren, Russell Walden, Jan Robertson and our editor, Anne French. For their support to Gillian through the period in which she was taking the photographs that appear here, we thank Jill and Tom Field, Rosemary and Roger Parr, Glenn Busch, Bruce Foster, Julian Bowron and especially Kevin O'Ryan. We are indebted to all those who allowed us to invade their buildings, and to the architects who designed them. For permission to quote an extract from *Landfall in Unknown Seas* we thank Allen Curnow and his publishers, Penguin Books Ltd. We are grateful for the permission of the copyright holders to use the photographs reproduced here. Except where otherwise noted, all the photographs in this book are by Gillian Chaplin and David Mitchell.

Finally, David is grateful for the influence of his most vividly remembered mentors – Vernon Brown, Bill Wilson and Peter Middleton, and offers special thanks to Julian Mitchell and Digby Fortescue for putting up with their father through several hectic months.

David Mitchell
Gillian Chaplin

Introduction

The 'elegant shed' could be just a catchy synonym for architecture: after all, the shed is a fundamental form of shelter, and elegance is one of the refinements we hope to find in that special class of shelters we call architecture. But most people do not naturally associate elegance with sheds, and they are inclined to think that anyone who does must have a primitive aesthetic sense, or a high-blown theory, or both.

Still, nobility of purpose is a poor yardstick of architecture. However much prestige we attach to the monuments of our culture, they are rarely more beautiful than the vernacular buildings we barely think about. At the ugly end of the scale there are not many New Zealand sheds as offensive to the eye as the big brick Anglican cathedral in Auckland, which was built with the most praiseworthy intentions. Of course we might expect to find a strong shed-building tradition in a country where people are proud of their pragmatism. The 'beauty which expresses function' (as John Berger put it) is more common here than the 'beauty which expresses hope'.

The functional tradition has produced a great many well-designed artifacts, especially for people who live in the outdoors: the bush singlet, the Swandri and the seaman's jersey, the Thermette, the Fairydown sleeping bag, the Trapper Nelson and Mountain Mule packs, the cattle stop and gumboot, the half-round letter box and half-round haybarn, the cowshed and shearing shed. But the city too can boast gadgets that are vivid emblems of settlement: the Galvaboard garage, the Hill's Hoist, and the rotary mower.

Among New Zealand architects pragmatism is still the most morally defensible critical position. Called to comment on their work, nine architects out of ten will say it is based in the practical, as if architecture were a superior kind of engineering. It is true that much architectural design in New Zealand is notable for the ingenuity and economy that it displays. But architecture is finally an art, and no amount of attention to the practicalities of shelter can replace that emotional charge that the more memorable buildings succeed in giving us. There can be no one who has not been moved in one way or another by certain buildings. Good or bad, we recognize architecture by its ability to invade our emotional world.

Why then is the shed – a product of engineering if ever there was – an important source of post-war architecture, and the elegant shed a mythical goal? Because only since the 1940s have our architects been able to consciously elevate the pragmatism of their people and make art of it.

Something embarrassingly titled 'coming to terms with being a New Zealander' was upheld as an enduring struggle by post-war analysts of the arts, eager to identify and praise national distinctiveness when they saw it expressed. The Second World War had made New Zealanders particularly aware of who and where they were, and in the sunshine years which followed they were keen to make their own habits and manners and experience the subjects of their art and architecture. Not that our architects were oblivious to the course of the Modern Movement in the European world. They tried to tie the purist principles of abstraction to their vehemently defended experience of life and art here. They set out to show that an architecture could be made from the humblest New Zealand traditions, that the simplest conception of the shed could be crossed with the more complex notion of the house as a homestead, that the spare structure of a basic shelter could be elaborated by the behaviour of people inside it. As the first generation of post-war architects began to turn simple shed-like buildings into real houses, the myth of the elegant shed took form and gained a hold in the architectural imagination.

There is scarcely a New Zealand architect who does not admire simple farm buildings, trampers' huts and old-style baches. Many will say they owe their best ideas to their experience of unpretentious buildings such as these. Some will attempt to recreate them, but the more interesting will reinterpret the ideas and forms of the architecture they know within the expectancy and opportunity of their own time. The architects whose work appears in this book have done at least that, though in this personal view of New Zealand architecture over forty years, some fine buildings and some excellent architects have had to be left out because their work has not fitted the story I have chosen to tell.

It is easy to see that some architects are more interested than others in that particular kind of architecture which is shed-like, yet elegant. Stan Ballinger, for instance, used some of the technology and a lot of the aesthetics of industrialization to make a Dunedin house that looks and performs like a high-tech shed. And in the late 1960s Jack Manning eschewed the sentimental and the picturesque in favour of a refined simplicity that was occasionally even mechanistic. But though few architects were unaffected by their admiration of utilitarian structures, some did not primarily aim to make elegant sheds. Many of the celebrated post-war buildings of Otago, Wellington and Canterbury referred back to the architecture of the High Victorian era. Miles Warren and Ian Athfield managed to combine in their own living rooms an evocation of the grandeur of upper-middle-class Victorian life with the austerity of mid-twentieth century construction. In each, a grand piano and an antique or two lent opulence to a lofty but essentially spartan room. One would be hard pressed to find a shed in their own houses, or even behind them, but the traditional shapes of rural buildings do appear in the houses they have designed for others. They appear too in the enchanted castles of Roger Walker. It is hardly surprising that among Walker's favourite buildings is a row of shearers' huts on the Gentle Annie Road between Taihape and Hawkes Bay. They are as complex, spiky and cheering as one of Walker's own architectural cocktails.

It is easy to confuse a liking for buildings which are functionally direct with simple nostalgia for the manners of an earlier time. Many of today's architects are luxuriating in a new tolerance for historicism and decoration. The elegance of their sheds is often of the applied kind. They are more frank than they used to be about admitting the sources of their work, and they are given to quoting bits of architectural history in their buildings. The history they are quoting is often other people's, and some of it is only a few years old: the 'global village' shares architectural ideas as rapidly as other kinds of information.

One might think these were tough times for the elegant shed. But every few years yet another architectural radical sets out to reinvent shelter from scratch, asking once more what would happen if we got rid of buildings altogether, and wrestling again with the temptations of technological daring on the one hand and cultural baggage on the other. Before long our fundamentalist inventor is living in the landscape with an armoury of electronic gadgetry, projecting holograms on clouds, studying hydroponics and trying to design an infinitely variable insulating fabric for making life-support suits out of. Those damned waterproof jerseys hang in the mind: they never seem quite adequate. For a glorious instant, though, the elimination of architecture seems possible. Then the cat stirs by the fire, and rain rushes the roof. Under the pohutukawas on the beach is a sodden Chesterfield suite. Paradise begins to look like a scene from *The Bed-Sitting Room*. Some kind of shelter seems to be necessary after all. Pretty soon the elegant shed is floating up in the mind's eye, distant and difficult and always just out of focus and just out of reach. But worth stretching for.

David Mitchell
Auckland, June 1984

Russell. The town is mostly distinguished by its history and its setting. New buildings on the waterfront are now given a Colonial flavour by ersatz decoration — tourists cannot tell the mock historic from the real thing.

1: Hometown New Zealand

If 'hometown New Zealand' means to you Greymouth or Hokitika, Coromandel or Thames, then you are lucky. Everyone likes quaint coastal gold towns, pretty little ports like Akaroa and Russell, towns set in scenic splendour like Arrowtown and Raetihi, and faded old resorts like Te Aroha and Hanmer, tinged with Edwardian grace.

But out on the Piako flatlands are Ngatea and Paeroa, and further south, Morrinsville. Cow towns, grown up on the crossroads or the railway siding. They look alike right down the country — Kaikohe, Bulls, Milton. These inland towns are the least picturesque, lacking the enchantment of a romantic past or a striking location, and that makes it easier to find in their unremarkable streets the mother lode of folk architecture in New Zealand.

The recurring form is of the main-street town, signalled by a scatter of light industrial sheds on the highway. Houses start near the 50 k.p.h. speed zone, and move out to flank the strip of shops that runs through the town centre, gap-toothed with parking lots and petrol stations. There are false fronts above the older shop verandahs, and occasionally a second floor to house the local dentist or lawyer. The street is punctuated by key buildings

Main street, Masterton. The main street of the New Zealand town is more convenient and is more fun with cars cruising through it, than it is blocked off as a pedestrian mall, sparsely populated, and generally crudely detailed.

that break its prevailing pattern: the once-dignified Post Office, the grand corner pub, the new supermarket. On the grassed corner is a roughcast Plunket Room and Women's Rest Room; up on the hill is an old wooden hospital set among the larger well-planted sections where the town gentry live.

It is easy to recognize this town, even to acknowledge that it is a complex and largely useful construction. But is it made of architecture?

At least since the Renaissance, architects have tried to view their work as a three-dimensional art. And in this century they have seen the quality and sequence of the rooms inside buildings and the places between them as the essential concerns of architecture. They identify the 'sense of space' in a building as the fundamental ingredient, as if architecture were habitable sculpture.

Within this frame, the small town as a formal whole makes adequate sense – whether, like Milton, it is built as two magnets held apart by the infinite road or, like Russell, it spills to the seashore, lies along the beach, embraces the bay.

Tui Co-operative Dairy Co. Early dairy factories rapidly picked up an identifiable image – as outsize gabled sheds with the front walls iced in two-tone roughcast.

Fish shop, Karangahape Road, Auckland. One of the finest pieces of window painting in the country, now destroyed. The painted window is rare in new fish shops, but murals on the inside walls depicting fishing boats and fishy scenes are still common.

But many of the buildings that make up the small town can hardly be seen as spatially distinguished. What is the new block of shops but a matrix of square metres, cut into lettable blocks? What is the upper floor of offices, but a sandwich of air, cross-hatched by stock partitioning that traces simple organizational diagrams? And what is the ordinary bungalow but one of a small set of near-standard plans on a floor set just 2.4 metres beneath a flat ceiling, the whole placed near the centre of a regular plot, and crowned with as weighty a roof as the owner can afford?

We might detect here a difference between the public and the professional perceptions of the vernacular. The common building stock is spatially undistinguished, but it can repeatedly be given distinction by decoration. Indeed, the less distinguished a building is in a three-dimensional sense, the more responsive it is to changes of decor and image. It is the very predictability of the vernacular that gives it currency, allows it to be accurately described and evaluated, to be readily bought and sold.

At different times, the hairdresser, dairy owner and greengrocer might all occupy the same space in reasonable comfort. Architectural concerns barely rate consideration against simple practical demands of floor area, location and rental. Yet there is a right way to present every shop, a style to be held, and an image to be pasted on the front.

Like pop music, the forms of pop architecture are predetermined. The architectural space is given, and all the distinction it receives comes from a concentration of decorative effort that is largely skin deep.

Nevertheless, the decorative language of architecture has strict rules that make the multiple functions of buildings comprehensible. In the 'ordinary' architecture of the New Zealand street there is a language we all understand. It is a pastiche, with sources that are mainly English or American, made unique by adaptation to the local culture.

The bloodstained bandage, abstracted in the striped barber's pole, came straight from England, but the sign in the window 'We mail to Hobart' was peculiar to New Zealand. It is only the greengrocer whose shop front is a roller door, whose walls are mirrors canted to double the display of fruit. Only the old fish shop has a painted window with gilded letters and pictures of the sea. And only the dairy has a window packed with advertisements, a Tip-Top sign on a corner wall, a waste basket hung on a pole, a row of newsflashes and magazine posters trapped in wire frames, a

12

The milk bar, the dairy, the superette and the supermarket suggest shades of functional distinction so fine that even locals have trouble identifying them exactly. The newspaper might be sold in any of them, but the supermarket rarely opens on Sundays, and the milk bar rarely sells butter.

tiny room jammed with islands of produce and lined to the ceiling with tins and packets and refrigerators.

The images of shops are changing a little all the time, even when their roles remain stable. The refrigerated window of the butcher's shop once had a tiled base to the street. There were tiles inside on the walls, and sawdust on the floor. Butchers wore aprons, striped in red and white – the colours of meat and hygiene. Now the butcher's shop is more often decked out in Formica and vinyl, mostly in red and white.

Colonel Sanders adopted the apron the butcher wore, and rendered it in painted stripes on the roofs of Kentucky Fried Chicken stores. Striped roofs in any colour thus came to signify takeaway chicken, and red and white stripes can now be found in food bars that sell all kinds of takeaways.

Under market pressure, competitors steal distinctive styles from successful traders. The dairy owners, threatened by the big supermarket, expand their stock a little, repaint their signs, and call their shop a superette. The man selling used cars steals from America some of the shrewdest devices in commercial architecture. He is the old horse trader brought up to date, and images of the old West flourish on used-car strips. As often as not there is a hitching rail to the nominal verandah on the front of the tiny hut that acts as a lookout for the dealer, perched on the back of his lot. There is a down-home air about it, designed to counter any unease that the dealer's white shoes might cause. The yard itself is always clearly defined texturally and spatially – by white pebbles spread on the ground or a distinctive tarseal, and by tents formed cheaply in eye-catching fluttering flags. The used-car boys are found on the edge of town, out on the commercial-industrial strip that many people see just as an ugly jangle of signs and wires. Yet even here, commercial pressure ensures that the road and its parts remain always visually coherent. It is laid out like a supermarket aisle: it is a monument to functionalism.

Along Barry's Point Road on Auckland's North Shore, the buildings are unimportant, just containers set behind signs. In the town planner's mind the front yards were perhaps meant to be landscaped, but they make too good a showplace for that. The main signs on the front boundaries are spaced to fit the pace of a passing car, and at 40 km/h the driver cannot miss a thing.

We used to navigate the highway by landmarks, looking for steeples and monuments poking over the hill. We took our bearings from the larger

Barry's Point Road, Auckland. A street almost entirely regulated by the opportunities and constraints of commerce.

objects around us. Now we do it by reading signs over motorways, and if we look about unduly, and steer in the direction we think we are going, then in a flash we find we are spiralling down some off-ramp that leads into the never-never.

One person's never-never is another person's home turf. The last turn-off from the motorway may lead to the most forgettable suburb, but even that is furnished with one of the great artefacts of mass culture – the New Zealand bungalow. Smart alecs may sneer at the staple Kiwi house, saying it is just like its neighbour, predictable and boring. But there is more variety in a New Zealand suburban street than in a Himalayan village, or a street of Sydney terrace houses. The detached family house is the world's favourite kind.

In every country, the house of the common people is a stock item, simply repeated. So in New Zealand the bungalow looks much the same from place to place, and shows little variety in internal subdivision. New Zealanders like a stable domestic life, and are slow to change the ways in which they provide for it. Mass housing is always a conservative industry, locked to patterns of planning, production and expectancy.

Anyone could recognize the standard plan of the New Zealand house. The front door is for strangers, who might be held at bay on the step. The back door is for family and friends. These doors connect relatively directly, and on one side of that connection are the 'living' quarters of the house, where guests are entertained, while on the other are the bedrooms. The kitchen, bathroom and laundry are grouped along one side wall near the back door.

This plan can be kinked into an L-shape, bent into a boomerang or raised above a basement. Internally, the bare volumes are similar from house to house, constrained by the flat ceiling at a height standardized by the building codes.

Charles Edwards, drawing house plans for Universal Homes, summarizes his task as 'shuffling little boxes into economic shapes'. The elements of the house have been predetermined by traditional patterns of behaviour and association, modified by economic limitation and social class.

The big builders of cheap houses compete with minor elements, chosen to produce marginal variations. A richer and more confident social group

Opotiki War Memorial. This is not an obelisk pointing to the sky, but a column of a kind used in Greece 2500 years ago for supporting buildings. What, then, does this column support? Is the classical column so rich in noble associations that it can be detached from its old physical function and given life on its own as a monument?

pioneers an innovation before it appears at the lower end of the house market. For example, the working family who once ate in the kitchen now prefer a dinette and a servery; the parents would like their bedroom to open into the family bathroom, in a down-market version of the 'en-suite' arrangements of the rich.

If the underlying elements of the mass house have stayed much the same, the picture it presents to the street has not. We intimately associate the image of our house with our conceptions of ourselves, just as most of us take some care over what we wear, and even over what we drive. We are extremely susceptible to the influence of fashions engineered by merchants sensitive to the anxieties of their clientele. Perhaps the instantly antique, neo-Colonial house owed its popularity in the late 1970s to that public taste for nostalgia that blossoms during periods of national economic insecurity.

The New Zealand house might be a relatively standard set of cells, but we

In the suburban street a minutiae of detail marks one house off from another.

fill it with a vast array of private possessions, and we treat the garden and the exterior surfaces with deliberation. The concise summaries of land agents are revealing. Whether speaking of a 'real Tudor with all the extras' on Nob Hill, or an 'ex-Statey' in the Dell, they isolate the key information their clients seek. House buyers are most concerned about where their possible home will be, what unnecessary but important features it will sport, and what it will look like. As anybody who has bought one will know, the single act that most sways a buyer to ignore or investigate a certain house is the first glance they get of it. They know in a flash whether the mask it wears is one they would like to live behind.

A Universal Home plan of 1964. This is close to the elemental plan of the post-war New Zealand house, and many houses of 1984 are still arranged in a similar way.

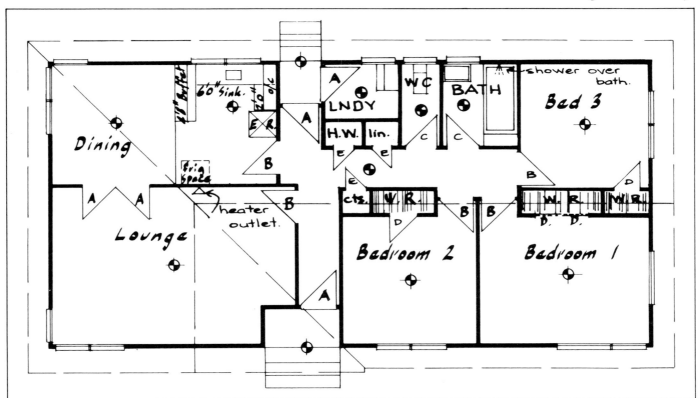

Archetypal bach on Rangitoto Island.

The major contributions to New Zealand architecture made by lay people might appear to be merely decorative, yet there are forms of building that have developed with little influence from the design professions. The functional tradition of farm buildings continues, with the new vaulted semicircular barn as beautiful in its efficiency as the old red shearing shed or musterer's hut. But if we are to seek common ground between the high architecture of the professional designer and the folk building of the amateur, we might most easily find it in the architecture of the bach or crib.

The simple pragmatism of the hut builder could be adopted with dignity by anyone setting out to make a holiday house – at least until about 1965, when the old bach began to be replaced in the real-estate advertisements, and on the sand dunes, with the fully blown holiday home.

The early bach was that straightforward cottage that is reinvented

everywhere in the world where a simple house is needed. It is rectangular in plan, with a gabled roof on rafters that can be extended to take lean-to additions. There is such a house a few miles north of Cape Horn (it is the southernmost in Tierra del Fuego), and one of the same shape and size at the entrance to Islington Bay on Rangitoto Island. The lonely pair who guard Argentina's most uninhabited waters hold a substantial arsenal in a house that might have kept a New Zealand family on holiday. Of course the simplest shelters are determined by available material and labour to an undue degree, but even they are set by the pattern of earlier models, locked as appropriate images in the culture.

OPPOSITE PAGE *Colonizing the dunes. A typical sequence from the Mount, near Tauranga. In the private realm there was at first the sun umbrella and the picnic blanket, then the tent, the caravan, the bach, the beach house. Now, tents and caravans are jammed into fenced compounds of unspeakable squalor, and the beach front is lined with holiday homes. Public services have been meagre by comparison: the beach road was first sealed and drained with kerbs and channels, and a row of Norfolk pines transformed it into a marine parade. In the 1930s a real marine parade was made along the Napier foreshore and it was a charming and particular kind of public park. Caroline Bay, with sound-shell and water dodgems was a beach park too. But most post-war beach reserves offer little more than a dank toilet block and a rubbish bin or two. The hub of the beach is the surf club house, propped above the dunes and roofed with a jaunty skillion like a monument to its progenitor, the 'dunetopper' bach.*

Pre-war baches on Rangitoto are being progressively demolished by the Hauraki Gulf Maritime Park Board. The Board is perhaps overzealous: as the island is returned to its 'natural' state a charming sample of our architectural heritage is destroyed.

At widely separated points in New Zealand there are communities of old cottages. At the Rakaia river mouth, at Taylor's Mistake, at Makara, at Stewart's Gully and Glink's Gully, and at many points on the coast and the lakes, miniature gabled cottages lie together as a family of forms, once taken for granted, but now picturesque.

During the late 1940s and 50s, when the effects of the war eased and optimism rose, a different bach became established – of as simple a form as could be imagined by a people who saw access to the natural riches of the country as a right available to every family. Fewer than one in ten families was ever to own the keys to bachland, the form of development that was to run like a bush fire down the most beautiful coasts, but the right to own a bach was unquestioned. Few realized that natural assets were most threatened by the facilities that were built to enable those assets to be enjoyed.

Across the Hauraki Plains and the Waikato, and down into the King Country, lived people who rarely saw the sea. From the tip of the Coromandel peninsula to East Cape the coast is cut off by mountains from the populated centre of the island. The railway to Thames took holiday-makers to that sheltered coast; buses ran to Waihi and Whangamata through the Karangahake Gorge, and to Mount Maunganui over the Mamakus. But it was not until the car became available to every middle-class family that the great surf beaches of the east coast fell within reach. Then, come summer, small-town businessmen left the closed suburbs where they had been penned for the winter in stout and muscle-bound brick bungalows, and drove with their families for the open coast, to camp high on the dunes in Fibrolite flimsies.

The new lean-to baches sprang simply from the road, their roofs reaching for the ocean. Landscape windows gawped across the Spinifex and ice plants at the baying surf. Behind each bach was a pair of corrugated iron

water tanks which within five years would weep with rust from the stress of salt wind. The new car was parked, uncovered, on the rising buffalo grass, and home-made paving slabs stepped hit-and-miss to the dunny out the back. If there were pines growing on the rectangle of sand then they were left to grow. If not, then none were planted.

The Dunetopper: a lean-to bach of the 1950s.

A Dunetopper, a Lantern-jaw and a Buck-tooth waiting for Christmas.

This desert camp, built by inland people from the close green hills, was no refuge from the hot sand and the beating summer day. It was a celebration of the open sky and ocean. The old lounge suite behind the picture window caught as wide and free a panorama as the site allowed. In the back end were the kitchenette and the kids' bedroom that was tight with bunks, jammed against the Pinex ceiling in an unholy fug. This house was a new kind of service mechanism – a machine for appreciating the view. For succour in the wet it had an old fridge full of booze, a drawer of Monopoly and cards, and a shelf of paperback thrillers.

Still standing along the dunes at Orewa, Whangamata, Waihi, the Mount and Ohope, and every 30-year-old sandhill colony, are lean-to baches, now old and touching veterans of the dunes, heavily painted in dozy timber, or bleached and blotchy in Fibrolite, lifting their lids to the sea and to the summer dreams of stock agents, secretaries and school teachers in walk shorts.

'Artist's impression', probably advertising a builder's house of the 1960s. Vogue details of the time are carefully and deliberately featured, such as exposed aggregate paving, a barbecue, and a section of translucent roofing. John Maynard coll.

The bach of the 1960s and 70s was rarely a mere Fibro weekender – more often it was a miniature family home, but because it was made to be used only during holidays there was a licence in its design that could not be tolerated back at the homestead. If the bach of 20 years before had been a lean-to dune-topper on the crest of the sandhill, this new generation of holiday homes was often obliged to fill a second rank of sections set back and below those on the beachfront. The bach was hoisted above a concrete-block basement finished crudely as a garage that doubled as a games room on wet days, or as a sleeping space for surplus guests. The balcony, long absent from the New Zealand house, reappeared in the lantern-jawed or buck-toothed beach house as a harbinger of the new hardware of outdoor living.

As if to bring life at the bach into the suburb, home owners began to develop their gardens as places of practical use. They flocked to retail garden centres and bought trees, paving slabs and cobbles, kitset glasshouses, shadehouses, pot plants, swimming pools, barbecues and outdoor furniture. Entire industries developed to satisfy the demands of the new lifestyle offered in magazines and television programmes. That uneasy relationship with the ground that had been the least engaging aspect of the post-war bungalow began to give way to a more intimate connection. The trade name 'Ranch-slider' made an apt myth of the revived association, but old-style french doors became popular too, as we tried to bring the inside out and the outside in.

NEXT PAGE Our place is in technicolour and the rest of the street is in black and white.

21

22

The popular house of the late 1970s looked back to our earliest European house style, the one we call New Zealand Colonial. But it was not a box of square rooms placed symmetrically about a corridor as the early house had been. Inside, it was not much different in layout from other post-war houses, although as bylaw controls changed to accommodate them, the attic bedrooms of the early cottage reappeared. While the neo-Colonial house, originally popularized by architects in the 1960s, is a meagre thing when it lacks a verandah or french doors, the essential ingredients of the style are very few: a criss-crossed balustrade almost anywhere, and a finial or two at the peak of the gable are enough to denote it.

If the house can be seen as a veiled box of artefacts, a packet of goodies wrapped plain or fancy according to taste, that is not to deny its more primal roles, or threaten its traditional status as a sacred place. But the image of home that we cultivate and carry has a pictorial face. It is the street view stretched across the full frontage of the suburban plot. 'Our place' is in Technicolor, and the rest of the street is in black and white.

Some people, of course, go further than most in personalizing their homes. One of the great folk decorators was Charlie Jackson, a Niue Islander who transformed the interior of a stock house in Auckland by painting walls, doors and ceilings. Mrs Jackson recalls that one day he simply began without warning, drawing images from his head and painting them straight onto the walls. Though Charlie has died, the Jackson family home, still painted and embellished with a substantial collection of family mementoes and photographs, is a vivid indication of how affecting a skin-deep decoration can be.

Mr Russell of Te Horo has never really finished building his house. It is made almost entirely of concrete: even the roof was boxed and poured in place, the wet concrete lifted from the ground in a bucket. Mr Russell deliberately varied the faces of his house, forming bays and recesses. 'It's what they call projection building,' he says. The simple shapes are further

PREVIOUS PAGE Charlie Jackson, shown on his front porch, combined his own home-made species of traditional butterfly decorations with interior wall paintings that owed nothing to established custom. He freely mixed figurative representation and abstract design.

Russell house, Te Horo. The flowers, of waste plastic, and flattened corrugated iron, do not merely mimic real plants as commercial plastic flowers do. Russell recognizes opportunities, and thinks as an artist.

NEXT PAGES Greek Orthodox Church, Masterton. While the form of the building is entirely traditional, the combination of local materials with the designers' inventions makes it unique.

broken down by a distinctive decorative style that formalizes and abstracts the jointing found in stone masonry, mixes in favourite emblems of the artist, and owes a little perhaps to the mock-Mayan decor that was popular in the 1930s. Yet the painting and modelling of the plaster is far too bright and idiosyncratic to be the work of a professional decorator. And the flowers he has made of flattened strips of corrugated iron on steel rod stems have been so popular he has had to plant them in the lawn only on special occasions: 'The bastards kept pinching them whenever I went away.'

Outside Masterton is a tiny Greek Orthodox Church that is partly a piece of folk art and partly a professional job. It is planned on a Greek cross, traditionally domed over the centre and arched above the arms. Outside, the roofing is an ingenious mix of flat metal plumbing and curved corrugated iron; within, the plaster-board walls are entirely covered by icons which are the painter Stephen Allwood's interpretation of traditional Byzantine

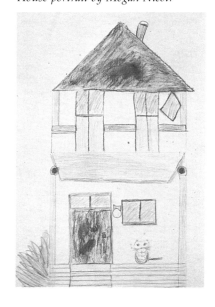

House portrait by Megan Nicol.

images. Allwood took a year off art school to do the work, producing probably the finest painted interior in the country. The building was supervised by George Pantelis, and built to serve just three Masterton families.

Some people would say that none of the folk building illustrated to this point was really architecture at all. Certainly it lies well outside the world that post-war architects here have imagined and tried to build. Most of them detest the standard Kiwi bungalow. They rebel against that sealed-up, insistent shape repeated through the suburbs in pastel hues, or beaming in brick and tile from a mown lawn in the midst of paddocks.

Since the war most architects have seen themselves as functionalists, taking part in the great world movement of Modern Architecture. They have tried to make buildings that were, above all, efficient. They have deplored decoration and anything pretentious or unnecessary. They have thought that the outside of a building should do no more than reflect the architecture of the interior. They have even believed that, given a little more education, nearly everyone would agree with them. But they have had a lot of trouble persuading a public that has known very well from the age of seven what a house was supposed to look like.

Redwood house, Orakei, by Vernon Brown, 1943. The white porch in the black house is like a bite out of a coconut. In construction and in detail Brown's buildings were utterly ordinary. He was more interested in shaping wholesome rooms which fitted the domestic patterns of his time and his social group. Auckland University Architecture Library.

2: The Auckland Style

To the general public of the 1940s, the most uncompromising modern houses looked like cowsheds. Ironically, to describe them so was to flatter their architects, who consciously strove for that functional basis for architecture which had been taken for granted by generations of farmers in building their cowsheds, shearing sheds and haybarns.

Immediately after the war the most influential architect in the country was Vernon Brown. He worked in Auckland for 20 years, and taught a generation of students at the Auckland School of Architecture. He explained the shed-like wooden houses he designed in strictly functional terms: 'All cant and humbug were avoided . . . The roof was low-pitched, because there is no snow in Arney Road.'

Connet Melville house, Epsom, by Vernon Brown, 1947. The bare essentials are the substance of the house, and the lean-to shape of the whole structure can be read from within it. Auckland University Architecture Library.

Low-pitched the roof might have been, but it was never flat on a Brown house: 'A flat roof was expensive and the owner had enough ground to walk about on without climbing onto the roof to take exercise.'

This tart tone was characteristic of Brown's utterances, which occasionally slipped into intolerance: 'There are too many leaky windows about today, and they're mostly of the casement variety. The most effective type of window is the high, double-hung sash stretching from the floor to the ceiling. One advantage is that it compels the messy-minded person to curtain her windows decently . . . '

Only a teacher who drew as well as Brown did could describe a student's drawing as 'an insult to the eyeball'. And only a person of his cultivation, intelligence and charm could have persuaded a good number of Remuera landowners to build the plain, strong, unostentatious houses that were this Englishman's interpretation of the principles of modernism applied to the place he had adopted, using the everyday materials he found there.

Brown's houses were typically of black creosoted boards with single-pitched roofs, and were undecorated except about the front door, which was generally set in a tiled porch. Where the black outside shape of the house was cut away by a patio or a porch, Brown painted it in white as if he were showing off the interior – like a coconut with a bite out of it. Inside, his houses were generous and relatively open in plan, and he took great care in the placing of windows, in the fall of light, and in the colours and tones of the surfaces. He had a subtle understanding of Munsell's colour theory, but his beguiling acceptance of ordinary building techniques and the casual geometries of his houses concealed the artifice that lay behind them: the Vernon Brown house looked for all the world like a big bach.

He had stepped into a country in which few artists had spent a long time searching for a distinctive voice that would not betray a dependence on England, but he quickly developed an architectural manner that was his own, though it barely showed on the few larger buildings he designed. Of these, the Auckland Glass Company building in Hobson Street, Auckland, was the most admired by architects, but the row of yacht club houses he designed at the Westhaven boat harbour were the most conspicuous. They had a self-consciously nautical air that was Moderne rather than modern, making them fashionable again in the early 1980s.

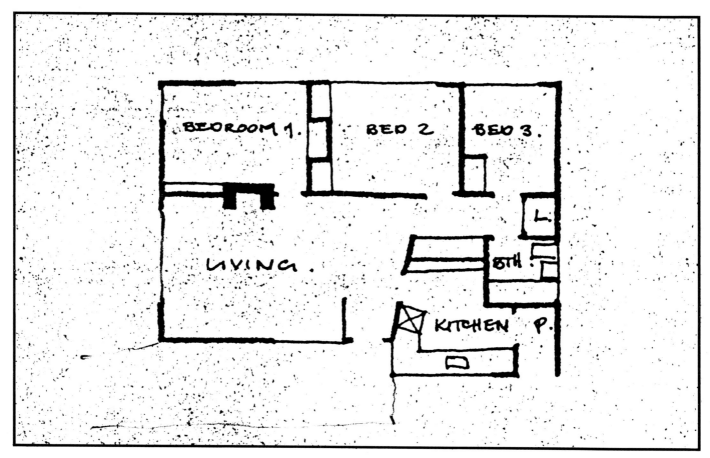

Brown himself was to attack vogue decor and short-lived fads: 'The basis of modern architecture is honesty – honesty in plan and materials. But it is confused with a fashion. It is being mixed up with clothes. If the best and most economical material offering is punga fronds, then one has a better chance of designing a modern functional structure with them than by importing some exotic method of construction . . . There are some weak, pretty-making people who call upon shutters and window boxes, but one cannot consider such things, any more than one can consider the American idea of painting flowers around the base of the house . . .'

Hofmann House, Remuera, by Vernon Brown, 1946. This plan sketched by Brown shows the direct way in which he arranged the rooms in a simple gabled house. The dining table folded down from the angled wall to 'save space'. The plan is economical to the point of being physically tight and socially demanding. Auckland University Architecture Library.

'Mr Brown's cowsheds' were not the only new houses of the 1940s to propose a New Zealand form of modernism. A similar directness and an enthusiasm for plain timber framing and big areas of glass that allowed strong links to the outdoors showed in the work of Rixtrott in Auckland, Pascoe in Christchurch, and Fearnley and Firth in Wellington. But Brown was persuasive and articulate, and through his position as a teacher was a prime influence on the first post-war generation of New Zealand architectural students. Many of them were returned servicemen. They had seen something of the world and they had high hopes for their lives back home. A few were to sweep the cause of modern architecture forward with a handful of succinct, innovative houses that they designed and built themselves on the North Shore of Auckland.

In the 'rehab' years that followed the war, New Zealanders were more united than at any time since – naturally conformist, supported by a continuation of the welfare services begun in 1938, their children given free milk and apples at school, free dental care, TB injections, X-rays, team sports and military drill. The brick and tiled bungalow was the most popular housing goal of the middle-class and the State house was a close approximation to it. Where the first pre-war State houses had been miniatures of the brick mansions of the rich, those of the late 1940s and 50s were more often rendered in weatherboard with coloured concrete roof tiles. Like all good mass houses, they were in no way remarkable. But they combined the minimum of utility with the minimum of dignity.

The State house provided facilities that were almost identical to those of the cheap house built by large house-building companies, yet it remained a last resort to most people who were looking for a home. No private house-builder mimicked the standard windows, the high sills or three-foot square porch of the State house, and none could afford to ignore the appearance of their house from the street with the unconcern displayed by the State house planners.

But it was not the unambiguous stamp of its origins that diminished the State house's appeal to the young architects of 1945. Most of them would have applauded the idea of State housing, provided that the State's architects had followed the principles the modernists in Europe had set down. Indeed, the early work of the State's Housing Division included some apartment buildings that might almost have been built in pre-war Europe, with a parentage that reached back to the Weissenhofseidlung exhibition of housing in Stuttgart in 1927, designed by Mies van der Rohe, le Corbusier, J. P. Oud and Walter Gropius.

When Gordon Wilson was Government Architect, apartments were built in Dixon Street, Wellington and Greys Avenue and Symonds Street, Auckland. Their designers were influenced by the ideas of an urbane and talented Viennese architect called Ernst Plischke, who worked for the State for ten years from 1939. But to the young firebrands who were architectural students in 1945, none of these buildings combined the principles of modernism with an appropriate respect for New Zealand manners. At least, that might have been their conclusion had they discussed them at all, but they were more concerned with their own projects.

A little band who called themselves, in various combinations, the Architectural Group, Group Architects and Group Construction, set about designing and building timber-crafted houses that were like hand-made models of houses that might have been built with machine standardization. The Group had earlier published a manifesto of noble goals: ' . . . only architecture can successfully arrange the background to our daily lives. Only noble human ends produce good architecture. The spirit of modern architecture must permeate the whole life of him who practises its skills . . . '

In 1950, led by Bill Wilson, this handful of enthusiasts built two houses on back sections in Takapuna. The houses were open-planned, with very little distinction between the kitchen and the dining area, which in both was

simply a part of the lounge. Such openness might be seen as symbolically appropriate in the house of the unified nuclear family – the open plan came to be vilified in the 1960s, when the family had become a less secure unit.

The 'total design' demanded in the Group's manifesto extended in these houses to the furniture and fittings, and even to an abstract mural painted by Tony Treadwell. The houses may have looked like models of the kind of functional, economical house the State could have built for Everyman, Everywoman and Everykid, but the mass-housing world largely ignored them. They remained brilliant, spare, athletic art works.

Then quite suddenly Auckland got one of its finest works of architecture – the studio-house designed by Bruce Rotherham for himself, and built by Group Construction in 1951. Here were the lean timber frames and the stiff, diagonally sarked planes one might have expected from a member of the Group. But the house was high and boxy, opened up with a daring 'curtain-wall' of sheer glass on the south side, and with glass doors and a solid flap of weatherboards to the garden. A brick shaft of fireplace, stair

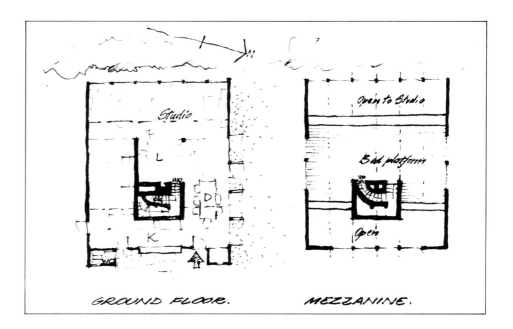

GROUND FLOOR.   MEZZANINE.

Rotherham house/studio plan, by Bruce Rotherham of Group Architects.

and organ-loft rose near the centre to subdivide the ground floor plan, and support a dish-like mezzanine sleeping platform. The lavatory opened off the back porch with the casualness of a summer holiday house. In its easy combination of 'natural' materials – the bricks and the flag-stoned floor – with the high and low spaces and varying viewpoints that the mezzanine allowed, the building pre-dated New Zealand architectural fashion by a clean 20 years. But Rotherham retained the adroit, summary planning that characterized his time: the wave of nostalgia that brought the 'snug' and the 'den' and the finial back into the houses of the 1970s was inconceivable in the halcyon days of 1951.

While the later houses of Group Architects were more complex and perhaps more subtle, none was as exciting, as new or as influential as the first few built between 1950 and 1955. The Mallitte house in Milford is a Group classic, occupied by the same family for 30 years. Designed by Bill Wilson, it has been left almost totally unaltered since it was built in 1954. The living areas are open-planned, but the children's bedrooms are separated from the parents' to give some privacy. The southern half of the

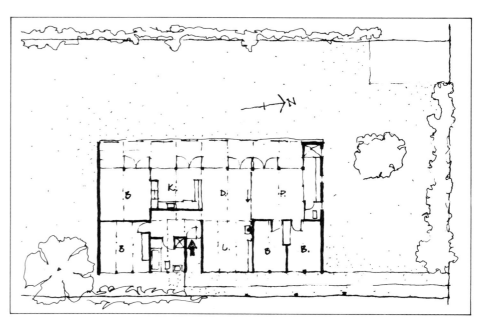

Mallitte house plan, by Bill Wilson of Group Architects. Compared with the work of their predecessors, Group Architects' early houses were highly systematized and relatively open.

gabled roof is kicked up at the ridge to form a clerestorey, giving sunlight to the cell-like bedrooms. That device was to reappear in the work of other architects, especially around Auckland, and so was the taste for exposed rafters and structural members that the Group refined to a high degree. As a contemporary, Miles Warren put it: 'When a 6" × 2" would do the job without sagging, then the Group used a 5" × 2".'

At least at the start, many of the Group's connections were with artists, intellectuals and socialists. It is perhaps still true that the farmer tends to live in the country as if it were suburbia, while the intellectual lives in suburbia as if it were the country. Certainly, for all their dislike of 'the tentacles of suburbia', the Group's houses were not urban. They were made to stand alone, as if in an unfenced Garden of Eden.

Living in the city was an art that had largely been lost since its heyday in the 1920s, when Grafton was a suburb and Symonds Street, Princes Street and Waterloo Quadrant were lined with houses and apartment buildings. The first really urban house to be built in Auckland since the war was the house Tony Mullan designed and had built for himself in St Paul's Street in 1958. It is now converted into an office, but its simple urbanity is still apparent.

Two Grafton houses of a few years later were designed by Peter Middleton and John Goldwater for their families – both were removed for the Grafton motorway. They were more like inner suburban houses, though Middleton's had the street wall and the closed courtyard of later town-houses. His house was famous too for breaking with modernist traditions and displaying some of the knick-knackery that Brown had found so offensive 20 years before. There were shutters to its more public windows, and the well-pitched cottage roof was trimmed with a finial on one gable end. (How that finial was to multiply through the houses of architects, and eventually through the mass housing stock.) Like Brown and Wilson, Middleton was an excellent teacher, a connoisseur of manners with a respect for the suburb that was unusual among architects.

Goldwater's family house was influenced by the peasant houses he had seen in Ibiza, and the availability and relative cheapness of concrete block at home. Goldwater built his own house of bare concrete block, with a timber roof frame covered in industrial Fibrolite. Even the two-storey verandah posts were of block. The heart of the house was a lofty family room with a

Middleton house, early 1960s. Peter Middleton was the first post-war architect here seriously to regard the suburb, the bungalow and the traditions and devices of popular building which architects had rejected. His critical insights were memorable, set in the intellectually soft climate of professional architecture. His own house, embracing forgotten traditions, secretly shocked his contemporaries, but influenced his students. Auckland University School of Architecture.

Goldwater house, Grafton. An early example of what is now called the 'family room', built around a substantial dining table. Here Goldwater elevates the fundamental activities of family life: his architecture is built around lasting rituals. John Goldwater.

Queen Street, 1925. The urban unity and vitality of Auckland's main street, photographed when the city suburbs barely stretched past Mt Eden, might be contrasted with the crudities of townscape which it offers today. The splendid building in the centre of the photograph, crowned with a dome, has recently been replaced by a truncated and banal office block occupied on its main floor by the Bank of New Zealand. The Bank's fine classical building over the road has meanwhile been reduced to a single street wall of stone propped up by an outsize new development behind it, in grotesque deference to the bare letter of the local council's preservation requirements.
Auckland Institute and Museum Library – Weekly News photograph

big dining table in the centre, and what might usually have been the Kiwi lounge was really a bed-sitting room for the parents. There was nothing prissy about Goldwater's work, nor anything indulgently pretty about his bare brick Synagogue and Community Centre for the Auckland Hebrew Congregation. That building is as direct and tough and wholesome as a loaf of fine rye bread eaten without butter.

Goldwater builds solid walled buildings and punches holes in them with a natural sense of judgement, controlling light and view. The Synagogue and Community Centre buildings stand locked in balance about a courtyard, above sloping walls of concrete against Myers Park like a bastion against anti-Semitism.

Together with JASMaD's International House, the Synagogue broke a dreary period in Auckland architecture. It had a European urbanity that was still foreign to Aucklanders in 1967, with a street wall that was scaled to respect its neighbours. Not that many learned from it. Downtown, developers palmed off a shady, windy quad as a public square. A pile of

West Plaza, by Price, Adams, Dodd.

*Synagogue and Community Centre for the
Auckland Hebrew Congregation, by John
Goldwater. The pagoda-like form of Early
Russian synagogues is echoed here. We
are reminded of that architectural strain
which stretches across to Finland and
appears in the 20th century work of Alvar
Aalto. But the plan, the volumes, and the
relations of the complex to street and park
are unique and admirable.*

grand Victorian brickwork that would have been revitalized in any civilized
city was battered down in the middle of town to make way for the brand
new squalor of the BNZ building.

And in 1984 a new breed of office block sits askew on every vacant street
corner. Townplanners have encouraged the amalgamation of small titles into
massive blocks, each covered by a two-storey podium from which a
free-standing office tower projects in a simple symbol of commercial
potency. Some of the practical ills of the Downtown complex have been
avoided, but the essential form of the built-up street has been progressively
eroded, and despite the dressing of Queen Street and Aotea Square by civic
gardeners, the centre of Auckland remains unlovely.

The office blocks of 1984 are all sheathed in the American vogue finish of
1974: mirror glass. The mirror building merely reflects its neighbours,
borrowing its subtlety from them and from the unpredictable play of light on
a multitude of mirrors. The architect can abdicate.

In sharp contrast, the last office block to give something sculptural to the city was the West Plaza building, by architects Price Adams Dodd. Built in 1975, its floor plan is almond-shaped, not unlike that of Gio Ponti's famous Pirelli Building in Milan. But unlike Pirelli's, it is striped vertically with fins on the long 'curved' walls. As one's viewpoint changes moving along the base of the building, the fins open and close together, making it a giant piece of Op art, and thrilling to look at from a moving car. In the most flattering sense, West Plaza might have been built anywhere in the world.

There has been little to mark out any other post-war office buildings as products of New Zealand, save for a paucity of expensive materials and a ham-fisted attitude to detail. Occasionally, the tight rein most developers try to hold on building costs allows that unencumbered elegance of structural expression which modernists the world over have sought to display. The collaboration of architects Warren and Mahoney with engineers Holmes, Wood, Poole and Johnstone produced, in the Union Company building of 1983 on Quay Street, a structure that offered its bones and sinew on the outside in a nicely judged display of the 'poetry of engineering', as we in the street know it.

Aesthetically, the Union building owed a good deal to the Pompidou Centre in Paris, by Piano and Rogers, but it is a machine of a different kind. It is perhaps more refined than the AMP building in Queen Street, but it represents international late-modernism in a local adaptation, just as AMP represented mainstream modernism 25 years earlier. To the designer, Jack Manning (then of Thorpe, Cutter, Pickmere and Douglas), AMP was a scaled-down Kiwi version of the glass skyscraper of America: 'Every architect working on office buildings at that time was in love with glass boxes.'

It was Manning who was co-ordinating architect and designer of several buildings in the redevelopment of Auckland Teachers' Colleges in Epsom. The group of designers, which included myself, worked through the late 1960s on a substantial collection of buildings strung out through a large holding of suburban land. There were elements of New Brutalism in the work, in which clear routes were set through the buildings and between them, to give order to the whole without relying on geometric uniformity and repetition (at the time, the chief ordering devices employed by architects). More obviously, though, the aesthetics of contemporary public and institutional buildings were rejected. The universities were building in exposed concrete, with concrete aggregate-panels used as sun-breakers, spandrels and necessary-looking decorations. The Teachers' Colleges

University of Auckland's Recreation Centre, by JASMaD. The gymnasium here is presented like a huge glazed house.

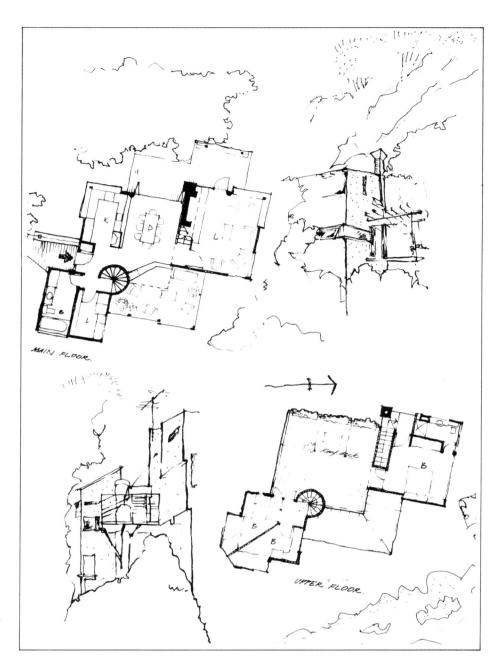

MAIN FLOOR.

UPPER FLOOR.

buildings were of timber-framed panels set in concrete frames, with the whole exterior sheathed in ordinary old flat Fibro, whooped up with gleaming sprayed polyurethane finishes, and screwed to the timber with stainless steel screws. The new austerity was hard-won, demanding careful detail and construction, but in the best buildings it gave the Cool Heroic style the architects sought. During the long construction programme, the later buildings were debased by countless changes not made by the designers, but the earlier work gets close to expressing the myth of architecture-as-mechanism that the architects worked for.

Geoff Haughey of KRTA made a mechanism from the workshop for straddle cranes that lift containers on the wharf. He designed an industrial jewel box that displays its insides to the waterfront drivers. In many ways it is a simple wharf shed, but this architect too knows the poetry of engineering. The straddle crane building is high drama passed off as simple practicality.

Even the Recreation Centre for the University of Auckland is a showcase. It is a big gymnasium designed by JASMaD to let the players look out and

the passers-by look in. There is no thump of boarding here, no reek of socks or air of punishment. Here sport is fun, and the building is friendly and house-like. JASMaD have often used the house form to embrace all kinds of functions, commonly capping even office buildings with big hipped roofs, and following a domestic style of detailing that is sometimes enlarged to stay in scale with larger buildings. There is occasionally a touch of Gulliver in it, but at its best JASMaD's work is approachable and familiar. Even the huge room in the Recreation Centre, with its carefully wrought timber rails and trim, owes a good deal to the post-war pioneers of domestic architecture in the Auckland style.

On the warm and gentle slopes of Auckland the easy open house is the one that fits the conceptions Aucklanders carry of themselves. One of the most open was the house Russell Withers designed for himself in the inland suburb of Glenfield in 1969. In essence, the house is simply a broken roof plane falling with the ground slope, propped above block walls that act as solid screens within it. There is the same risky reliance on craftsmanship and timber engineering that Rotherham and the Group had shown, but the house has a lightness that is spatially intrinsic, maintained by continuous glazing below the roof plane, and by a rigorous grammar in which structure and infill are always separated and always legible. With its nods to Frank Lloyd Wright, system building, craftsmanship and social tolerance, this house speaks more about architecture than about housing. It is the kind of optimistic tour-de-force that only a young and gifted architect could have produced. (Withers' second house was a solid villa, in radical reaction to the first.)

One way or another, the best Auckland houses make the most of the easy climate there. Several architects have designed houses in which they tried to ease the transition between inside and out, like Marshall Cook's 1979 design for the Osbornes, which makes subtle connections between the heart of the house and the benign outdoors. The principal intermediary is a garden room that opens over a wide frontage to the exterior on one long side, and to the interior living room on the other. In the 1980s it is fashionable to place heat-absorbing conservatories on the sunny sides of houses in a bid to harness solar energy, but the heat trapped in a north-facing conservatory

TOP, OPPOSITE
Withers house, Glenfield,
by Russell Withers.

BOTTOM, OPPOSITE
Osborne house, by Marshall Cook. Like
the Withers and Walford houses, the
Osborne house makes a dramatic play of
the relation between house and garden.

rapidly makes it uninhabitable for plants or humans. The Osborne conservatory faces south, and the house can be sealed from it by closing doors on cold nights.

In the house I designed for the Walfords in 1978, I varied the climatic controls of parts of the house to encourage the owners to move about it and vary the pattern of room use according to the seasons. The idea is considerably extended in a 1982 project by Nigel Cook.

There are not many closed gardens along the 16-kilometre sea frontage of Auckland's east coast. From the front stalls of the North Shore suburbs you look across a garden formed of the seashore to the water and islands of the Hauraki Gulf. On a tongue of lava at Black Rock are three houses that could be found together only in Auckland.

Swan Railley Paterson designed a house entirely clad on the open seaward side in mirror glass, set on the faces of curved tiers which progressively step back as the huge house rises. Built in 1984, the house is utterly compelling and downright foreign. As if in mischief, the undulations of mirror glass break up reflections of Rangitoto – the volcanic island Aucklanders have chosen as a tribal emblem. These curved silver walls are utterly captivating, but like sunglasses on a face they give nothing away: the goggling stroller on the shore might be staring without knowing it straight into the eyes of the owner. The house appears as a vast stage set for a play that we plebeians can only guess at.

Mrs Firth, who lives in a tiny bach-like house beneath the mirror wall is pleased with her new neighbour: 'The whole back of my house has got much brighter since the mirror house was built,' she says. Her kitchen is

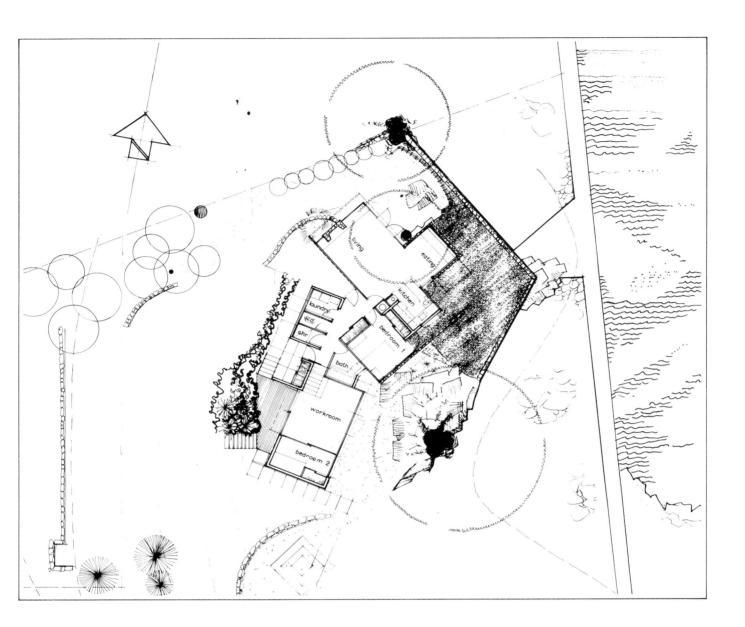

now blessed with light from the south, and her back garden is bathed with a beneficent glow from next door. Hers is a charming cottage with additions by Imi Porsolt. Down in front, the old french doors open simply to the sun from a living room we might remember from childhood holidays at the beach. In rooms like this we sit back and look out, or face one another, bathed in light from the side and in the continuous sound of the sea.

Mike Austin was perhaps responding to memories like that when he designed the third house in this row, built for Win Chapple in 1969. Austin has said that his client was looking for something straightforward – 'like a collection of army huts' – and pleasant though that image was to him, he had a leaning towards the work of Frank Lloyd Wright. The house does not look like a group of army huts designed by Wright, however. It is an engaging cottage, shrewdly planned around a big pohutukawa on a rock, with irregularities of form and an ordinariness of detail that are so beguiling they appear almost accidental. Even the picturesqueness of stone wall, picture window and storm shutter appears casual and unselfconscious. Like an old bach, the Chapple house lifts its cap to the Gulf view, and spreads itself under the pohutukawa. If there is one vision of paradise that Auckland architects share, that is it.

Christ's College dining hall designed by Cecil Wood, and well-known to post-war architects Miles Warren and Peter Beaven.

3: The Christ's College Connection

Though Christchurch touches the sea, it is essentially an inland city, and an inward-looking city. It is built on flat ground. There is no distant view to celebrate, and the outlook of every building must be constructed. Christchurch is a city of squares and parks, and walled gardens.

A few Christchurch architects dabbled with the shallow-roofed bach style of house that Aucklanders had popularized within the architectural

47

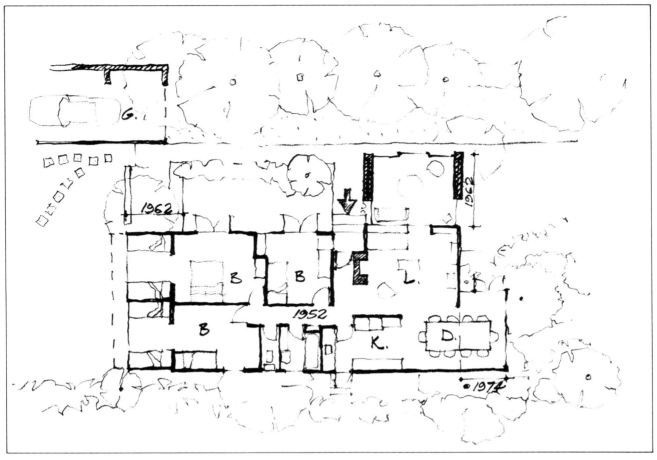

Donnithorne house plan by Don Donnithorne.

profession. But there was no lasting conviction in their efforts. It was not
that Christchurch lacked a bach culture of its own. Nearby were the baches
of Banks Peninsula, the miniaturized houses of Stewart's Gully, the shacks
of Birdling's Flat, and the cave houses of Taylor's Mistake. At the Selwyn
river mouth there was a settlement of fishermen's huts and fences in
bleached boards and corrugated iron that could have inspired a regionalist
architect, and even a local style, had anyone chosen to mythologize it.

No one did. It could be said that Auckland architects had taken possession
of the bach as a source, forcing southern regionalists to look elsewhere. But
there were more deep-seated reasons too. Where the houses of Wellington
stand long-legged on hill-faces that are carpeted continuously in green and
yellow, and the houses of Auckland lie to the sun and the sea, those of
Christchurch are keyed to their plots and to the private realm of lawn and
garden and court.

The peaked roof announces the cottage behind the wall, and the
two-storeyed house, found often along the plush edges of the Avon and
Hagley Park, stands confidently looking into the wider domain of the park.
In the inland matrix of hedge and wall, the low, shallow-roofed one-storey
house has no presence. It is reclusive.

Yet there is more reason still to reject the bach as a source for Canterbury
architecture. Neither the rich nor those who looked for their roots in
England could accept it as an appropriate model for their homestead or city
house. Wherever it appears in New Zealand the house that is formed like a
bach or a shed is almost always designed by an educated liberal for people
of similar kind. Canterbury architects, forever reminded of the Englishness
of their city, and of their own high architectural heritage, warmed more to
the model of the steep-roofed English cottage.

While early Christchurch modernists, like Pascoe and Hall, had largely ignored any pressure to be regionalist and locally distinctive, the strongest and most influential post-war architects in Christchurch sought, in their houses at least, a modern interpretation of the European house. Christchurch was already well-stocked with cottages built through the first half of this century, but the work of post-war architects was tempered by a knowledge of contemporary Scandinavian and English housing.

The house which Don Donnithorne designed for his family in 1952 looked as if the Swedish architect Markelius might have sketched it out. It was a steep-roofed shingled cottage, sheathed in board and batten (an uncommon material in Christchurch houses, though it is featured on one of the city's most popular buildings – the Antigua boat sheds). The plan yielded no surprises, splitting the functions of sleeping, serving and living in the relatively predictable fashion of the day. Yet the house caught the attention of other architects. It was sweetly proportioned, distinctive but unassertive, homely but true to the principles of modernism. Could it have been the prelude to a new regional manner – a Christchurch style?

In hindsight, pictures of the Donnithorne house may have had more influence on architects outside Christchurch, than the real thing had on local professionals. Although it never quite set a stylistic evolutionary line in Christchurch architecture, the house, now carrying three lean-to additions, is gracious, unpretentious, and glows inside like a polished chestnut.

In the late 1950s two old boys of Christ's College, Peter Beaven and Miles Warren, strode into the architectural world of Christchurch, and within a few years became established as the pace-setters of the city. Each had admired a different aspect of the architecture of their old school. Beaven was a maverick romantic, and Warren a restrained classicist.

Miles Warren had returned from London in 1955, after working in the

Donnithorne house photographed in 1952. A simple adaptation of the open plan and the shed form to the restrained traditions of Christchurch, the plan offering a little more privacy than its Auckland counterpart and the roof steepened to suggest a cottage. Donnithorne family.

*Donnithorne house in 1984. Now
tempered by lean-to additions and a
luxuriant garden.*

architectural division of the London County Council during a period in
which the LCC was producing some of the most skilled and influential
housing design in the world. The buildings Warren had worked on were
part of major housing projects at Roehampton that were models of
conscientious English town-planning crossed with the grand and
simple-minded planning principles of the great Swiss architect Le Corbusier.
Roehampton was a softened slice of Le Corbusier's visionary city 'La Ville
Radieuse', built before the vision was fully realized at Brasilia, the capital of
Brazil.

Warren was excited by the work of the New Brutalist architects of Britain,
by what he calls 'their bread and butter' attitude to architecture, and by the
aesthetic they developed that was based on making explicit the ways in
which their buildings were put together. That elemental attitude was not
entirely new. Aesthetically, its foundations had been laid before 1920 by
Gerrit Rietveld, and de Stijl and the artists of Constructivism.

In the 1950s no architect could approve the functional limitations of the
red and blue and black chair that Rietveld had designed in 1917. Yet it
displayed the articulation of parts that Brutalists like Warren sought in their
buildings, and the systematic repetition of elements that modern architects
saw as appropriate to their machine age.

Warren hauled the formal complexities of Constructivism into line by
designing within regular building systems that constrained and ordered his
buildings. Regular geometries, of course, have a life of their own, and
buildings based on them can fit their uses as uneasily as Rietveld's chair did.

At the university hostel of Christchurch College, Warren and Mahoney
fitted the student rooms within a geometrically disciplined framework of
concrete and block in a way that might have come from the egalitarian

OPPOSITE
*(Top) Chair designed by Rietveld. Such
colour arrangement is close to the
contemporary paintings of Mondrian and
will not be found in much New Brutalist
architecture, but the elemental clarity of
this chair might be fairly taken as a model
of the consistent systems architects like
Miles Warren expect their buildings to
display. The aesthetic route from
Mondrian and Rietveld to Warren is long
and complex, involving other important
figures like Le Corbusier and Peter and
Alison Smithson. It is modified by other
traditions too, but the constructivist bias
is still clear.*

*(Bottom) Christchurch College, by
Warren and Mahoney. 'The College never
called itself a hostel!' said Warren,
pinpointing exactly the way in which
these residential buildings for university
students are seen, at least by those who
administer them. The chapel is a very
subtle translation of Gothic intention
within the vocabulary that the architects
introduced to Christchurch in the 1960s.*

50

Christchurch College Chapel.

attitude we generally approve in housing peers. In that sense, the building is correct. It clarifies its brief. Further, despite a military air, it evokes the English residential university college with its courtyard layout even if the courts are larger and greener than those at Oxford or Cambridge. This is the Colonial response to an English model that still wins applause in Christchurch, and here it is very well executed.

In Auckland though, the University Student Union by Warren and Mahoney fits its frame less happily. In the classical language of the architects, the layout of walls and openings must acknowledge the regular spacing of columns and beams. In a building with many functions this is no easy constraint to comply with. It unduly forces patterns of movement, and regularizes room types and sizes. The building frequently fails to fit its functions, and remains always a little uncomfortable. Here too, the Constructivist aesthetic becomes insistent. The endless clarification of elements becomes a kind of featurism, and the repeated module a tyranny.

A host of fellow travellers took up the more obvious characteristics of Warren and Mahoney architecture – the white concrete block panels in unpainted precast concrete frames, the steep metal roofs, and the manner of joining all elements so that each was distinct by making a negative recess between any two parts of the building that made contact. By the mid-1960s the Christchurch style was firmly set, and in the hands of some, Constructivism had become an obsession. The feature stair was likely then to have a feature rail held by feature brackets with feature screws.

Warren and Mahoney were to become the best known, and arguably the most popular, architects of the 1960s and 70s. Yet their most influential building was one of their first; the little single-person flats set in a row in

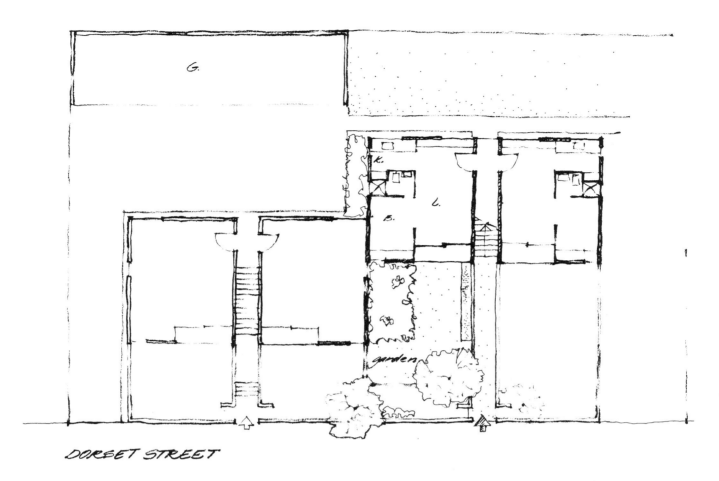

DORSET STREET

ABOVE AND NEXT PAGE
ABOVE AND NEXT PAGE
*Plan and photographs of Dorset Street
Flats, by Warren and Mahoney. The most
influential building of its time in New
Zealand. As if to sheet home the
advantages of such a building type, Miles
Warren himself lived for a time in one of
the flats, and developed the garden as a
delightful outdoor room formed within its
block walls.*

Dorset Street, Christchurch, in 1959 gave substance to a vision of the
town-house that was to capture the imagination of New Zealand architects
and clients alike.

The underlying model for these flats was the English terrace house, but
because the flats were very small, one was placed above another so that each
pair overlooked a courtyard. Stairs between groups of flats gave access to
those on the upper level. The architects here declined to use a continuous
balcony to give access to the upper flats, and thereby avoided the squalid
connotations of the 'sausage flats' that were being built at the time in city
suburbs elsewhere. Warren and Mahoney have often used this method of
access to the upper floors of all sorts of buildings, avoiding corridors and
continuous balconies at all costs. The technique can be seen in Christchurch
College, at the University Student Union building in Auckland, and at
Christ's College.

At Dorset Street the architects were blessed with a site that was shallow
and wide, ideally suited to a row-house development, but it was not until
1963 that they got the chance to show what could be done on a large deep
site with a relatively narrow frontage. Three 'flats', as they were still called,
were built for Mrs Broderick in Merivale, and these were truly what we now
know as town-houses. At that time many commentators were still asserting
that New Zealanders would not live in flats, but within a few years planning
ordinances around the country were adjusted to allow the kinds of buildings
that Warren and Mahoney had demonstrated could be pleasant, private and
popular.

If the best Auckland architecture of the 1950s was produced with socialist
fervour, that could hardly be said of the new architecture of Christchurch.

Lyttelton Road Tunnel Building, by Peter Beaven. Here sculptural expression outweighs constructional rationality. The consistency of parts of the building is largely visual: the 'solid' walls are of stucco, and the supporting sticks are of concrete, elaborately formed to look simple and systematic.

The Christ's College old boys who led the renascence came from well-heeled families, and were happy to accept that architecture was a naturally expensive prerogative of the rich. Yet another old boy of Christ's, Cecil Wood, had hired the young Warren not long after he had left school, and Wood's respect for good architectural manners rubbed off on his pupil.

Peter Beaven was the foil to Warren for nearly twenty years, as brilliant and as erratic as a torched box of fireworks. To the first four ships that brought settlers to Canterbury, Beaven added, in the form of the Lyttelton Road Tunnel building, a metaphorical fifth ship, tethered to the tunnel mouth, high and dry on the Port Hills. The toll booths were shaped as a row of gondolas, or gun-boats perhaps for the sheriffs of the tunnel, who strode down to their vessels on a grand stair from the mothership. The building may be an overblown celebration of the rather ordinary task of administering a relatively minor hole through a hill, but it has been designed with sustained aplomb. Here Beaven was carried and cued by the civic pride Christchurch felt in its new tunnel in 1964 and he played to the vanity of the smartly uniformed tunnel-keepers too. Now that the fanfare has died, they shelter within it like fugitives.

Where Warren and Mahoney are inclined to simplify and categorize functions and forms, Beaven strives to make them complex, to fractionalize them, and to find within each architectural task distinctions that can be displayed in the fabric of the building.

When he was called on to renovate and add to some old buildings owned by the Canterbury Building Society in Auckland, he seized the chance to show that intricacy and richness could be developed from scratch and that the qualities he admired in the Italian streetscape could be adapted to fit a New Zealand city. In a virtuoso display of planning skills he punched a staggered arcade through several buildings from Queen Street to High

Canterbury Arcade and office building, by Peter Beaven. The tiny office building is fully glazed to the floor and the ceiling on each level, with daring openings in french doors alternated with double-hung sashes. That gives it a unique sense of generosity, which is enriched by fins, shutters and balconies giving a depth to the front wall which we associate with old European buildings.

Street, and linked it to a tiny shaft of offices that was wedged between existing buildings encrusted with balconies and shutters and crowned with garrets.

There was a kind of determinism about it. Could the bustle of a European city be generated by the architecture with which it was associated? Certainly the arcade drew traffic, and in 1967 when old Auckland arcades were quite dead it led to a revival of them in Auckland and elsewhere. Other parts of the project were influential too. The little office building legitimized historicism. Beaven happily plundered the traditions of any culture that suited him, displaying an attitude that became increasingly acceptable to other architects of the 1970s. He fixed a band of glass into the new verandah roof built onto the old building on Queen Street and started among architects a passion for glass shop verandahs.

Habitat, by Beaven, Hunt and Reynolds. This is an architecture of controlled picturesqueness and skilfully concealed artifice.

In the 1980s, Warren and Mahoney have made the verandah a two-storey contraption in curved glass, allowing first-floor shops and restaurants to look down beneath it into the street, and affording a view up from the pavement to the faces of the high buildings and the sky above. Not that the glass shop verandah is entirely of our time. Once, verandahs in Christchurch were often made of metal sheet bent to a curve and set in iron tees; and there is a verandah still, opposite the Bridge of Remembrance, where heavily painted glass panes, peeling in places, are set in the curved fan above the street corner.

If Beaven's pastiche in Auckland was his most complex and mannered exercise, the building at Queen Elizabeth II Park for the Commonwealth Games of 1974 was his biggest. Beaven Hunt Associates designed the building with the engineers Lovell-Smith and Sullivan and Associates, placing two grandstands back to back, one facing a vast enclosure with two pools in it, the other facing the track and field oval. This splendid shed is a huge social and physical mechanism, a building of big straightforward gestures, that celebrates both sport and its own grand engineering. Its effects batter the senses, the surfaces of water forever glaring with quicksilver reflections, the whole hall filled with the continuously bounced sounds of screaming spectators or swimming children and the thump of diving boards recoiling. Here, sensations not in themselves pleasant contribute to the power of the building. The place would be smaller without them.

When Peter Beaven left New Zealand to live in England he had not long finished (in association with Burwell Hunt and Keith Reynolds), a medium-density housing scheme on steep ground in Thorndon, Wellington. In summary, it was probably the best development of its kind in the country with the first stage finished in 1972. The house units were interwoven with great complexity, yet they retained the sense of being discrete parts of a specific village. Habitat, as the project was called, mimicked the collisions and adaptations that occur over generations of vernacular housing in Europe. Beaven had made a construct of the kind of English town he admired, and within it he had worked the variations of form and detail he thought were physically necessary, keeping a constant eye on pictorial possibilities. His respect for English traditions might be dismissed as simple snobbery, were it not for his remarkable ability to persuade with the vibrancy and richness of his work.

That talent is clear in commercial buildings too. The Manchester Unity office block in Christchurch is shrewdly patterned enough on the outside to entertain the passer-by without compelling attention. And even the Ramada Inn (later called the Vacation Hotel) has, in its striped service shafts and tipped roofs, enough zest to mute the vulgarities of the facade.

Beaven has managed to combine in his work the purist principles of modernism with all those qualities that purist modernists dismissed – a passionate respect for tradition, a penchant for trumping up 'richness' by gratuitously modelling facades, even a taste for nostalgia and an eagerness to flirt with the picturesque. In spirit he was probably our first post-modernist.

T & G Triangle Shopping Complex by Warren and Mahoney. The glazed double-height verandahs work as well at night as by day. Instead of looking out to the busy street from inside, we look at night from the dark outdoors into the glittering interior.

The idea of the 'big room' was popular with the Victorians. It fitted their expansive view, and they built town halls all over New Zealand, even in towns as small as Otorohanga. Now there is a new wave of town hall building, with new halls in Wellington and Christchurch, and a proposal for Auckland.

Of these three, Christchurch has the best. There, Warren and Mahoney knew the social and physical setting precisely. The Avon was

Queen Elizabeth II Park, by Beaven Hunt Associates, and Lovell-Smith and Sullivan and Associates. This is robust, direct architecture in which the designers have taken a consistent attitude to the solution of problems big and small. The huge roof trusses which stretch from side to side appear on the outside of the building, each individually roofed with a long tunnel vault of corrugated iron. The ducts of the ventilation system appear as exposed innards threaded through the structure. In this space big items like diving towers and control booths are simply plugged in like fittings and furniture, and substantial service areas are lost beneath the grandstand seating. There is enough 'slack' in the structural envelope to accommodate a great number of social and physical services, from offices and toilets and changing rooms and staircases, to pipes and ducts and wires and machinery. In such spacious public enclosures as this, structure and skin and services can be treated as separate elements to be combined additively, where in small structures, especially houses, they are intimately related and many items are multi-functional.

acknowledged, but not deferred to, the two halls and the restaurant were all distinctive and wholesome rooms, and luxury was implied in details of polished brass and unassertive marble. In Wellington, however, the usual Warren and Mahoney clarity is absent. Outside, the main hall is ringed with glazed accessways, designed to enliven its massive walls, but the looping stainless frames around the foyer and glazed sections fit the rest badly, and the building feels as though it is straining to impress. In the streetscape, the Christchurch hall is an opportunity, and the Wellington hall is an obstacle. But in Auckland, where the City Council's architects have resisted any competition for the design of the proposed building, the little-publicized proposal is for a building that is without eloquence of any sort.

The Christchurch style was really the style of Miles Warren. The constructional elements of concrete frame, block panel infill, and spiky roof had appeared in his work by 1960, to be picked up by others in Christchurch and elsewhere through the 1960s. Hard-core modernists from Auckland rejected the wilful pattern-making that Warren employed in composing the exterior views of his buildings. ('Facade' was a term no self-respecting architect could have used.) But by the 1970s the flights of fancy that Ian Athfield was to display in Wellington made Warren's crimes against functionalist dogma look mild indeed.

Christchurch Town Hall, by Warren and Mahoney. There was no post-war civic style with any presence in New Zealand before Warren and Mahoney set one with this building. (The Wanganui War Memorial Hall, it will be remembered, was an aesthetic graft that failed to reproduce here.) It is a sign of our discomfort with civic dignity that we are still hard pressed to find a single public building here with a decent front door.

Massey house, by Plischke and Firth. The modernity of Massey house is striking compared with its neighbours in this perspective drawing by the architects made before it was built. Terence E. R. Hodgson.

4: The Architecture of Display

The Wellington series of paintings Don Peebles made in the 1960s evokes the *place*. Wellington is condensed and vivid – you ride towards it to the thrilling sound of wheels on rails, or lift your foot and coast your car down through the gorge, or bank over an airstrip that is caught between hills and sea. Any way you come to it, the first sight quickens the pulse.

Wellington cannot help showing off its architecture. It is thrown up on the faces of the steep hills, where multi-storey houses appear to stand on one another's shoulders, turned like flowers to the sun. Even the boxy stucco State houses high above the Hutt Road take an heroic stance against the sky.

The city always offered a chance for the spectacular, but architects rarely capitalized on it with intent before 1970. The office of the Government Architect has been influential, but not always for the better. It produced some excellent housing and conscientious neighbourhood planning in the 1940s under Gordon Wilson, and during the 1950s and 60s some strong and appropriate control buildings at hydro-electric stations were built by the

OPPOSITE TOP
Massey house in 1984: The building has been extended and has become part of a continuous wall of city building which is as aesthetically consistent as any in the country. In the commercial mode of the 1960s, these buildings are respectful of one another and of the formal tradition of the city street.

State and designed in an office architecturally headed by Chris Vallenduuk. But there has been a great deal of mediocre and muddled architecture produced within the leviathan of the Ministry of Works and Development, and few works of real distinction, even in Wellington.

New Zealand architects have nibbled endlessly at the design of the small house, and in Wellington succinct and economical houses were designed in the 1940s and 50s by Cedric Firth, Ernst Plischke, Charles Fearnley, Tony

BOTTOM OPPOSITE, AND THIS PAGE
Futuna Chapel, by John Scott. Compared with the Wanganui War Memorial Hall, Futuna was intimate, approachable and architecturally of our culture. But it was not only distinctively ours; Futuna was mature and resonant and bigger than a house – the only other post-war building type we had made in our own image.

Treadwell and Bill Toomath. But there was no clear, regional distinction in Wellington architecture until the 1970s. The early post-war work still used the Auckland vocabulary, although Plischke, a Viennese architect, stamped his houses with the cool elegance of the International Style. A distinctive style is not a prerequisite of useful or even inspiring architecture, but it is a banner critics and historians search for, believing that where there's smoke, there's fire.

In the Sutch house, Plischke got closest to an Antipodean interpretation of modernism as the Bauhaus had taught it. Like the work of Marcel Breuer and Richard Neutra in America and Harry Seidler in Australia, it seemed as clean and pure in photograph as the European model. But in wider views, a double-storey section compromised the pure form. Neither the shape of the house, nor the New Zealand details, felt quite true to the modernist canon, as if the New Zealand zeitgeist had blurred it.

Nor was Plischke's finest public building quite authentic. Massey House, designed by Plischke and Firth and built in 1957, was Wellington's first celebrated modern office building. Plischke originally intended it to observe the classical form that had in different ways been adopted by contemporaries like Mies van der Rohe and Le Corbusier: the ground floor was to be as open as possible, showing the columns on which the building was to stand uncluttered, as if the footpath were extended beneath it. The concrete frame reappeared at roof level above the curtain walls, finishing the building with some free-form additions about the lift machines that evoked the concrete roof gardens of Le Corbusier.

The grand car showroom designed for the ground floor became instead the bookshop of Roy Parsons. In it a curved stair rose free of the regular geometry of structure to a mezzanine. Such spatial interpenetrations were typical of the modern way – the Auckland City Art Gallery had a similar refined stair and mezzanine built almost at the same time.

Even before Massey House had been built, Greenhough, Smith and Newman had designed the Wanganui War Memorial Hall, a building which paid scrupulous respect to the principles of international modernism. In this immaculate monument to the post-war spirit, a town hall and concert chamber (that in capacity almost match those of Auckland) are lifted on columns above an inset ground floor to float above a paved forecourt, faced in solid and pierced block screens, and painted in purest white. There can be few, if any, public buildings of the 1950s so indulgently sculptural and functionally 'wasteful' of space. The bare court that formed a setting for the building has rarely been as full as on opening day, but it was only nominally intended to be useful. Where most war memorial halls had been house-shaped, placed in suburban fashion behind an ennobling patch of lawn edged in standard roses, or bunged in behind a sealed parking lot, the Wanganui Hall commanded a site whose prime function was merely to give the building air.

The architects, working in England at the time New Brutalism was being born there, referred instead in their building to the Royal Festival Hall of 1951, to the Stockholm Town Hall and to the work of Oscar Niemeyer in Brazil, who juxtaposed white planes of concrete with tropical greenery. Further back, Le Corbusier's Villa Savoie – grand, calm and white, propped in a French field – lay behind every architect's vision of the building as an art object, set apart, floating free.

At Wanganui a lopsided dome pokes through the roof 'like a mound seen beyond a Wanganui river terrace', as Gordon Smith puts it. (Such images fuelled the imagination of the architects.) And from the air, the composition of the building reads like a Ben Nicholson painting.

All these connotations were known by the designers, consciously or dimly, as they strove to give form to the goals that modern architects embraced around the world, but their contemporaries at home could not accept so international an interpretation of modern ideals as the building

they produced. Nor could New Zealand architects easily accommodate the
work of talented Europeans like Henry Kulka and Gerhard Rosenberg in
Auckland, or Ernst Plischke in Wellington. Perhaps they were too
self-consciously nationalistic for that, feeling they had to develop their own
way of doing things. After all, New Zealanders still applaud the
made-in-New Zealand look with all the clamour of the unconfident, and the
search for a national style is restarted each time an overseas critic flies in.

In the political climate of 1939 Plischke had not easily been accepted here,
and his architecture was admired but not imitated by his New Zealand
colleagues. He was unsuccessful in his application for a professorship at the
Auckland School of Architecture, and in 1963 returned to Vienna, just as the
world of architecture here began to buzz with news of a religious building in
Wellington designed by a New Zealand-born architect called John Scott. It
was a chapel built by the lay brothers of a Roman Catholic Retreat, helped
by their architect.

Scott had been a member of Group Architects in Auckland in the 1950s,
but had shifted back to his Hawkes Bay home to practise. Like Ivan Juriss,
perhaps the Group's great craftsman both as architect and builder, Scott
respected material and process, even when his work was being built by lay
people. The floor at Futuna Chapel is of irregular slabs of serpentine brought
from the West Coast, set in a broad matrix of plain concrete, now glowing
with the patina and polish of 20 years. But it is not just the detail at Futuna
that impresses. The arms of the cross that customarily appears in a Christian
church are here lifted above the floor to form the faces of lofty triangular
wall planes, which look out to the four corners and take light through
abstract stained windows designed by Jim Allen to fit the geometry of the
building.

The central space is set about a high post from which the steep roof planes
are propped, and is closed around with low plastered walls at the roof edge.
Scott skilfully balanced opposites: the building is lofty but close,
outward-looking viewed from outside but centred when seen from within,
apparently symmetrical in three dimensions but on examination not *quite*
symmetrical. In all, it is lucid on the outside but inside has an unwordly
presence touched with mystery and awe.

The greatest religious building in modern architecture was built almost at
the same time as Futuna, but they were hardly alike. Le Corbusier's
pilgrimage chapel at Ronchamp in France looks more like Ian Athfield's

ABOVE *Athfield house with Ernst Plischke and Ian Athfield, 1975. The roof of the Athfield house is an artificial landscape of the same painted plaster that forms the walls of the house. The usual sensuousness of Athfield's buildings comes partly from the shapes he employs and partly from the continuity of the hand-plastered skins which form the surfaces of many of his buildings. Ernst Plischke, seen here peering at an Athfield porthole, could never have dreamed of this building: his work was precise, considered and refined by comparison. Ian Athfield.*

LEFT *Athfield House in 1969. The original section of house has now been added to, but the fully-blown architectural flamboyance of Athfield was clear in this early picture. Ian Athfield.*

'Fort Nyte'. The childhood hut of the compulsive architect Roger Walker. Photographer – the architect's mother.

dramatic Wadestown family house-cum-office than Scott's chapel. Scott used the materials from which any New Zealander might build a house, while Athfield made a house with a sequence of rooms that looked and felt European.

The Athfield domain runs from the Onslow Arms – an old bulding that has been further aged stylistically by the architect to resemble a nineteenth-century hotel – up a goat track to the new white palace on the bluff. When the house was first built and occupied it resembled no other building in New Zealand. Concrete block and wire on studs had been rudely plastered and painted white inside and out in a continuous surface that came from the ground to cover walls and ceilings and finally roofs. There were creamy balustrades and 'caves of ice', portholes that probed the sky, and windows that launched the eye in a dizzying gaze to the railway track down on the harbour edge, or picture-framed the harbour and the hills beyond.

In a single stride Athfield had left the shelter of New Zealand neo-Colonialism in which he had briefly lingered, and piled up a house that was singularly arresting and deliberately conspicuous. If anything, it looked as though it had been built by Mediterranean peasants, but its real means of construction and the life within it were distinctively Kiwi.

Athfield is interested in process as much as product, and he likes the owners of the buildings he designs to take part in building them. He claims to have started building work on his own house with few drawings. In the 16 years of gradual construction it has become, at least in its outlying areas, a collection of rooms which change function as the family or the architect's office grows or shrinks. But simple functionalism has never appealed to

Athfield. At their best his buildings are risky and rhetorical. As we crawl through a tube into a sleeping chamber in the Athfield house we are likely to wonder what bedrooms are really for. Athfield, of course, knows that good planning only counts when nothing more is offered. Nevertheless, there is a traditionalist lurking inside his flamboyant personality, and the living room, with outsize paintings and grand piano, Eames chair and rocker, emanates a baronial air.

Later, Athfield was to blend his Mediterranean plasterwork with neo-Colonial forms. In the meantime, another architect had become established in Wellington – a man of Gothic tastes and great architectural courage. Roger Walker was a refugee from Hamilton who designed and built his first building at the age of ten. Had Fort Nyte been an ordinary kid's hut it might not be worth mentioning, but it was a multi-storey job, visually broken into sections and decorated with a shaky spire. The visual language of Fort Nyte was remarkably similar to the one Walker was later to use in designing the Wellington Club building on The Terrace for Calder, Fowler and Styles. And, like the Wellington Club, Fort Nyte had a sign reading 'Girls Keep Out'.

For the Club Walker produced a Gothic concrete cottage that appropriately showed nothing but disdain for the functionalist lore of modernism. Walker miniaturized and complicated his buildings to an unprecedented degree, decorating them with extremely proportioned elements lifted from the vocabulary of Colonial New Zealand. The Wellington Club was built in a street where some of the dreariest buildings in the country had gone up during the 1960s and 70s. There were hundreds of thousands of square metres of offices shrouded in the vogue pattern of whatever day it was they were built. They made The Terrace look like an

Athfield house in 1984. This exquisite work room is one of the most freely formed in the Athfield house and it is deliciously embellished by the vine which is planted at the darker end so it spreads towards the light.

The Britten house, by Roger Walker. A virtuoso set-piece in which the architect's dexterity is nicely matched by the hopes and confidence of his clients.

advertisement against modern architecture. In this context, the Wellington Club was at once genteel and frivolous, bristling with 'features' like a pop temple.

Three years later, in 1974, Walker managed with the help of three builders and two extraordinary clients to build a house that cascaded down a rugged bushy hill so perilously steep that there was only room for a tiny landing at the front door. The house for the Brittens was built of many tiny rooms that were independently roofed, linked horizontally and vertically on ten main levels in a manner so complex that it was remarkable that the architect could draw the whole thing for the builders, let alone visualize it. According to Des Britten, he and his wife Lorraine would never have asked Roger Walker to design them a house, unless they had believed he would produce something extraordinary.

The Britten house makes original propositions about the idea of a 'house'. It suggests that a house might be a multiplicity of mainly private spaces, with larger social spaces provided elsewhere. That matches the Britten lifestyle – the two are restaurateurs who seek refuge at home from their public life.

With so much complexity in a single house, it was hard to see how Walker would handle 30 in one block. He was not deterred. A year after the Britten house, Park Mews was built. It was a pop assemblage of Colonial peaks and Walker circles. The last thing Walker could let any building of his design say was 'this is a block of flats'. So Park Mews looks like a huge Walker house (although a Walker house looks like a string of minute flats to some).

The personal architectural styles of Walker and Athfield have had great public appeal, and have been adopted by other architects. It may have been Middleton who reintroduced the finial to New Zealand architecture, but it was Athfield and Walker who used it – as part of an armoury of Colonial devices that included criss-crossed verandah railing, panelled french doors, attic rooms, dormer windows and curved verandah roofs, to which were added contemporary grace-strokes like round windows set in pipes, high metal flues and white chimneys. By 1975 the neo-Colonial style introduced by Athfield and Walker in the late 1960s had become fashionable to the middle class. No self-respecting architect could use the colonial language without translating it, modifying it or commenting on it architecturally, but

The Oaks, by Warren and Mahoney, is spatially the most pleasing arcade in the country, extraordinarily gracious inside.

the commercial world and the public at large showed no such reticence. Wood turners and demolition yards peddled new pine mouldings and balusters to match the old, and the Colonial house, new or old, became the most popular on the market.

In Auckland, Les Harvey had virtually done up a whole Parnell street in a mock-Colonial manner, and it was a raging commercial success. All around the country new shopping blocks were dolled up in Colonial garb, and even out on the mass housing estates whole streets were veneered in the Colonial style like sets in nineteenth-century television dramas.

That celebration of the particular, that rejection of the institutional or the repetitive which characterizes the architecture of both Walker and Athfield has not yet been successfully expressed in any large public building. It is of course difficult to express particularization in big buildings with large spaces or functionally similar elements, though there are models for it. At the turn of the century the great Catalan architect Gaudi achieved a sensuous personalized architecture that is occasionally echoed in Athfield's work, and contemporary Japanese architects have made big iconic buildings which suggest that Walker too could apply his skill with witty pop vulgarities to large city structures. So far, Walker's only work in central Wellington that does not have domestic overtones is the little James Cook arcade. It may be uneasy in decorative detail, as if the architect were trying to go half-straight, but it splendidly reveals the monumental massing of the James Cook Hotel towering over the glass roof of the arcade.

The transformation of central Wellington in the ten years since 1975 has been much trumpeted, especially by city politicians. The thrilling urbanity of the place is produced by a difficult topography that forces development into a small area, densely built-up around a curving hillside and an irregular street pattern – and it is sustained by an architecture that struts and parades with a glitter and arrogance unmatched anywhere else in the country. The

James Cook Arcade, by Roger Walker, trades quite directly on the spectacular Wellington skyline, framing it as if through tinted spectacles.

showy manner was set by Jellicoe Towers on The Terrace – as slender an apartment building as I would care to occupy, but in its pencil-thin proportions a fine piece of architectural brinkmanship designed by Allan Wild.

Most of the new office buildings are as mediocre as their counterparts in Auckland, but jammed together as they are of necessity, they are mercifully less obvious. Nevertheless, a few have been designed with panache, and the effect of them, added to the scintillating new arcades and glass verandahs, is so exciting that one barely notices the undistinguished work.

The glassiest and classiest shopping arcade in Wellington is The Oaks, by Warren and Mahoney. Externally, it is ringed with glass verandahs which look a little goofy cranked off a building that is only two storeys high. Inside, though, the tapering glass-roofed arcade evokes a street from Romanesque Italy in its spatial structure, and the mobility generated by the varying width of the covered street is reinforced by free-standing escalators that rise to an upper gallery. From there one can look back into the long white space of the arcade, and out from the surrounding shops under the

The Physics and Engineering Laboratories for the DSIR at Gracefield, by Structon Group.

glass verandah onto the encircling pavement bustling with pedestrians. No other public space in the recent commercial architecture of New Zealand capitalizes quite so thoroughly on the opportunities at ground level that a city block offers.

In the keen climate of Wellington the mirror-glass crystal sparkles. The silver building is in command, sharp and strong as quartz, and clearly more lively than the building made of black concrete aggregate or dark glass. Most of us do not give a fig what goes on inside office buldings, but we walk past them daily, and what they look like outside matters.

Bigger buildings are likely to go up in Wellington, but in the meantime the BNZ building – the biggest in New Zealand – overpowers all, just as the World Trade Center overpowers the great buildings of New York. The BNZ is like a cigarette packet among matchboxes. The walls are splendidly sheer, seamlessly detailed by Stephenson and Turner, but the blackness of them sucks up the light so that the building feels sinister.

Next door, the CML building is lean and clean, its mirror walls inflected with understated shuffles and lightly canted facets. Ross Brown masterminds such monuments from the Structon office (the same office that once produced the crudities of the New Zealand Racing Conference building, or 'Horse House' as it is known to architects). There are no spatial wonders in CML except in the outside shape, but it honours a fundamental demand of the city building – that it sustain the form of street.

Out on the flatlands of Gracefield is a Structon building full of DSIR laboratories and architectural jokes. It looks like some scientific device, as if it were an enlargement of one of the laboratory machines that might be found inside it. The Physics and Engineering Laboratories were built in 1982, and are a service network for pipes, wires and people. The plan arrangement is repetitive and diagrammatic, and the legibility of the entire building depends on the code of colours, numbers and signwriting. Here, the lessons of the motorway have been brought inside – we negotiate the corridors by reading signs rather than by recognizing features in the building. During the war we made timber-framed Fibro sheds for the kind of job the building at Gracefield performs, but this new shed is as showy as a space station, its complexities simplified as if they had been sorted and ordered by a computer.

Structon's work is the antithesis of the free-wheeling ad hoc constructions of Walker and Athfield. The lack of personal detail in Structon's buildings is a general hallmark of the work of big architectural offices, particularly when the buildings they design are large. While the personal and the idiosyncratic are usually valued in architecture, especially in New Zealand, cool repetitive buildings can also generate an emotional charge. The finest city skyscrapers have proved that.

The systematized buildings of Structon have been built in the twentieth-century global vernacular that it is currently fashionable to deride. A cartoon vision of the modern city persists in the public imagination: of giant building blocks with graph paper drawn over them, banal and uniform corporate symbols that reduce the man and woman in the street. In the CML building and the Gracefield Laboratories it is this very cliché that the architects manipulate, making expressive architecture of grids, and finding poetry in systems.

The reconstruction of central Wellington has been carried out during the later phases and the dying stages of the Modern Movement in architecture, not a time in which great examples are likely to be found. The early houses of Walker and Athfield, though, were delineators of a new age, and are a great deal more important in the history of architecture than any of the public and commercial buildings of the inner city. That is fine for architecture, and as the influence of the high artists has been fed down through the common stock, it may have been fine for building too. But the buildings of downtown are known to us all, and it perhaps matters more that they express the spirit of our time and excite us as public monuments. Can one conclude then that the recent architecture of central Wellington is unsuccessful?

The dignity of Massey House, the vigour of the James Cook Hotel and the glamour of the CML building are the highpoints in the largely undistinguished story of post-war Wellington office building. The success of concrete Brutalism in Christchurch led to a spate of unlovable concrete buildings in Wellington and elsewhere. Yet for all that, central Wellington is more exciting than ever. The Modern Movement produced a skin-and-bones style of architecture that was appropriate to the problems of mass and scale faced by developing twentieth-century cities.

Down the open streets of Auckland, graph-papered office towers look dumb and exposed. In Queen Street, the counterpart of Wellington's CML is

The towers of the black BNZ building by Stephenson and Turner, and the silver CML by Structon.

a vast concrete cheese grater that fails to live up to the opportunity its corner site offers. Where buildings stand apart, real set-pieces are invited, but in the close streets of Wellington a decent commercial norm will do, spiced occasionally with a show-off that can be dramatized – as the James Cook Hotel is by the glass arcade below it on the Quay.

In 30 years no New Zealand city has produced an urban architecture that can match the confidence and gusto of Wellington's. The general success of it is measured only indirectly by the responses of architects and business people, caught in the endless struggle for compromise between commerce and art. More telling is the real enthusiasm displayed for it by people in the street.

St Paul's Cathedral addition by McCoy and Wixon. The cross hanging in coloured acrylic is compelling, and the addition is thorough and honourable, but perhaps not as strong as even a literal completion of the cathedral 'in style' might have been.

5: Buildings Against the Landscape

The Scots settlers of Dunedin built to last. Like all immigrant groups they brought with them the building methods of their birthplace and turned the resources of their new country to purposes they had been accustomed to. They built in stone when they could afford it and brick when they could not. There were the fine building stones of Leith and Oamaru to be quarried, and the settlers built 40 brickworks in a city where now there is one. Dunedin was the fastest-growing and richest centre in New Zealand during the gold-rush years of the nineteenth century; now, as it fades, many of the splendid architectural symbols of its prosperity feel barely inhabited. But the masonry tradition lingers.

Oamaru stone, cut into blocks with power saws, is still used as a sheathing for houses in Otago, with the stone veneer tied back to a stud frame. Architect Ted McCoy has wryly observed that 'some people prefer concrete block to Oamaru stone – it's dearer.' McCoy himself is at ease making buildings faced in stone. As a Dunedin boy he retained a secret love of the Victorian buildings of his city through the period of his architectural education in Auckland, when modernism was all and Victorian architecture was seen as vulgar, pretentious and dishonest. To McCoy the main lessons of architecture were 'all there to be seen and responded to'. The 'positive, sculptural qualities' he admires in Victorian work are the strongest characteristics of his own architecture.

In a sculptural sense, his addition to St Paul's Cathedral was largely predetermined. The task of completing a prominent city monument is

The Hocken Building, University of Otago, by McCoy and Wixon. This is Victorian in spirit, like some of the work of Warren and Mahoney and Ian Athfield, but rendered in the materials of the day, for the purposes of the day.

particularly daunting when the old building is as grandly presented and as thoroughly assembled as the neo-Gothic St Paul's. McCoy formed an unspectacular apsidal end to the nave, of concrete faced in Oamaru stone between high concrete frames which did not mimic the stone ribs of the old building so much as reinterpret their task within the common techniques of 1970. The addition is sympathetic rather than seamless, admirably controlled in shape and material, but it falls a little short of sustaining the emotional pitch of the old nave, let alone of forming a climax to it.

McCoy and Wixon have since designed two buildings in Dunedin that refer strongly to the forms of Victorian architecture. They are of bare concrete, but like the best Christchurch work they lack the tawdriness that is so often found in the blotchy and mossy concrete of the north. The Hocken building of 1980, set behind the main open space of the University, houses several of its Arts departments, its Law School and the Hocken Library. In the cityscape of Dunedin it is a very large building. At first glance, the play of textures across the high concrete walls, the regular metal windows and the concrete grid appear as just the stock elements of mid-century architecture. But from the hills above the city one looks straight down onto North Dunedin and sees in it something quite unexpected: the Hocken building appears as a row of outsize Victorian terrace houses. Around it and nearby are real nineteenth-century buildings, tiny by comparison, but undeniably of the same ancestry. The building is driven to fit the formal compulsions of the architects, its internal arrangement dislocated a little as floor by floor it accommodates the towers and crosslinks that are its substance. Eleven stories up, each shaft is topped with a sloping Victorian roof covered in asbestos-cement slates that look like the real slates on the little old buildings below. Dunedin, the home of the terrace house in New Zealand, is the only city where the Hocken building could be understood.

Given his respect for the old architecture of the place, it is hardly surprising to find that McCoy has developed a regional style that is as clear as the styles of Christchurch and Wellington. Unlike the other cities, Dunedin has not much contemporary work in the regional style, and McCoy and Wixon, largely unsupported in their attempt to bring the qualities of Victorian architecture to their own work, occasionally slip into a

Alexandra Post Office by McCoy and Wixon.

picturesqueness that is only superficially agreeable. The Alexandra Post Office, with steep roof and walls sheathed in local stone, might seem an appropriate reminder of the old buildings of Central Otago, but the connection is purely pictorial. The building feels overblown, as if the architect were pandering unnecessarily to the public yearning for instant antiquity. We wonder what the staff are doing, apparently bunked down in the attic on a hot summer day.

Mrs Whitaker's house in Alexandra, by Francis Whitaker, 1979. There is an easy acceptance of timber building here that more closely resembles a twentieth century vernacular than the 'stone' Post Office down the road.

In more than one sense, a post office is an invitation to flag-raising. The functions of post offices have barely changed in fifty years – that in itself makes them good indicators of architectural fashion. Around 1975 energy conservation and respect for the context of a building were important issues in architecture. It must have pleased environmentalists to see the Alexandra Post Office rising stone by stone. The strong sub-structure was veneered with shapes and materials that seemed environmentally sympathetic, though none of the Alexandra buildings of the last 60 years look a bit like it. Perhaps the main disadvantage of the contextualist line on architecture is that the architect is encouraged to act as if nothing has happened in a hundred years, messing about with stonework to please the neighbours.

Essentially, McCoy is a modernist, and his best buildings accommodate traditions rather than ape them. The simple power of the new buildings McCoy and Wixon have designed at Otago Boys' High School is enough to establish them as a presence beside the grandiloquent stone walls and tower of the old school, designed a hundred years before by R. A. Lawson. That the new buildings are faced in the same crushed stone that appears in blocks on the old school is merely a nicety: it barely shows. It is the form of the buildings as solid objects that dominates. They do not spring from the ground; they sit on it with the weight of Stonehenge. Like the Hocken building, the classroom blocks are broken into vertical segments with external balconies running past one face of the classrooms between stair towers, allowing the rooms themselves to be glazed on both sides, greatly assisting the lighting and the view from inside. Such buildings would seem inconceivable in Auckland, where flimsiness is so easily accepted that some architects see it as a virtue. (Seeking a high performance from the least material has been an important goal in the bid to make the elegant shed.)

Otago Boys' High School additions by McCoy and Wixon. The traditions of masonry building in Dunedin are represented here in a group of concrete buildings with great presence. Even a random sample of children who go to school here spoke favourably about these buildings.

Even in Dunedin, the home of stone, there are flimsy-looking buildings. The Otago Harbour Board head office by Mason and Wales, built in 1982, is a mirror-glass slab with a silver metal topknot, parked between wharves hard on the water's edge. It literally reflects the ships that dock near it, so that seamen on the bridge see their ship approaching port. That is a gracious gesture. Occasionally someone who has not seen themselves for a week or more will get their first glimpse in the distorting mirror of the seaward face of this building.

It is perched over the water on piles. That is the way harbour boards build these days – on the harbour. It is the cheapest land they can find, and no one else is allowed to build on it. The Auckland Harbour Board is putting up its new office block on a set of giant legs on Princes Wharf – just as borough councils are apt to put up their council chambers on the local park. Architecturally, the Otago building would be little different were it set back on its sealed forecourt off the water. Either way, the least we could expect of it was that it contribute to our appreciation of the harbour, and of the relationships buildings can make with it and the opportunities they can offer.

Otago Harbour Board Head Office Building by Mason and Wales. The sister building at Bluff by the same architects makes much more of its mirror glass sheathing than this over-praised Institute of Architects award-winner.

The Auckland Ferry Building lives up to that demand. Arcaded on the ground floor, it encourages the public to use that rich realm that can always be found where the sea joins the land. The Otago building might briefly fascinate outsiders coming ashore, but it does not reveal itself and its occupants at all. There is no 'conversation' between the building and the world. Nothing can be seen of the interior save a dim view of the backs of furniture and fittings pushed against the mirror wall as if it were a blindfold, or the cure-all of the day. It is not that the idea of mirror walls is innately wrong, but they demand a response from architects that makes the most of what they have to offer: cutting the crystal to throw back at us an unexpected insight, kinking the wall to make a telling juxtaposition, or undulating it to distort and charm.

Only an architect with a strong will and a clear vision can build a tinny, thin building with conviction among the brick cottages, the white plastered bungalows trimmed and founded in brick, and the triple-decker, green and white, Otago-and-Southland sponge cakes of Dunedin. Stan Ballinger had the will for the task, and he demanded a lot of his clients too, when he

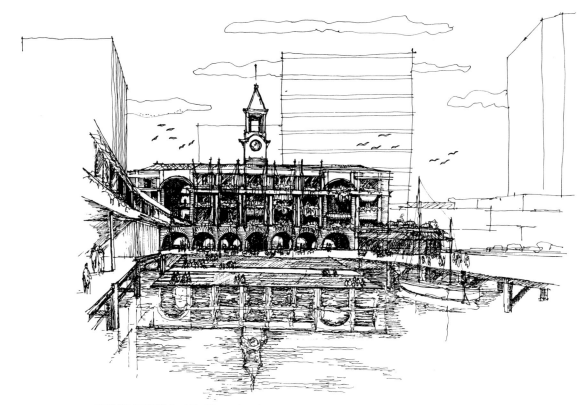

RENOVATION OF THE AUCKLAND FERRY BUILDING
MANNING/MITCHELL. ARCHITECTS
AUGUST 1983

proposed the house that the Morgans built in Andersons Bay in 1960.
Ballinger flew in the upper atmosphere of architecture, his functionalism so
pure and light that it floated above the turgid traditions of the brick and
stone city.

According to Frankie Morgan, 'Stan wanted the first house in New
Zealand that was dust-proof and fly-proof. He lived in utter discomfort
himself but he was very aesthetically involved. He was so thin and cold that
he made the place too damn hot. The kids got ribbed by their friends when
the house was first built, but when I said we might sell it recently, my
daughter was horrified.'

What was so outrageous about the Morgans' house? Mainly, that it was
made out of aluminium. At least, nearly everything you could see inside and
out was finished in aluminium. Underneath was the same old stud frame
that the rest of New Zealand had been built of. The Morgan house had flat
aluminium sheets slightly bowed on the outside walls, an aluminium roof,
double-glazed aluminium windows, and even an aluminium ceiling. It
looked as though Ballinger was a 'performance' freak. Even the cupboard
doors in this house were just thin biscuits of hardboard, stiffened on one
edge by their hinges, and on the other by a riveted aluminium angle that
acted as a door pull and had been pressed specially for the job. The house
had virtually no walls. Upstairs, where the parents slept, the main living
spaces were subdivided by folding doors, demountable bookcases and
cupboards framed in slotted steel angle. The undercarriage of the
cabinetwork was the kind of metalwork you see in locked storerooms and
unpopulated warehouses.

In Auckland, Group Architects had developed the minimalist aesthetic in
their early houses, but in the public mind their functionalism was tempered
by conspicuous craftsmanship: their buildings were full of exposed timber
that had often been hand-shaped. Ballinger was not remotely interested in
knots and grain. If something was made of wood he covered it or painted it.
It might be thought that he was insensitive to the world of the emotions. Far
from it: he knew the parameters of comfort, and he appreciated aesthetics
on that level which makes an art of physics.

When their house was nearly built, the Morgans – too poor to finish it –
'felt terrible', according to Frankie Morgan. 'We just gritted our teeth. The
windows on the front leaked like a sieve, and my husband and I remade
them on the living room floor. It took nine or ten years to recover.' Few

Morgan house in 1984.

people are as frank as the Morgans about the problems of their house, nor as aware of its grace. Frankie Morgan says: 'Stan's vision was substantiated by our performance. If we hadn't performed it would have been a disaster . . . but the client has a responsibility too.'

Frankie Morgan knows that the best architecture is made by people who take risks, trying to make art of what seems to be obvious, or accepting conditions like rationality-at-all-costs, that might make an owner's life uncomfortable and an architect's life worthwhile. In the search for the

Johnny Jones's whaling station on the coast north of Dunedin is an elegant shed of the nineteenth century. The tinned galvanized iron on these roofs might be among the oldest surviving metal roofing in New Zealand. This corrugated iron is stamped with the label of a company that changed its name in 1851, and the screws that fix a good deal of it pre-date the lead-head nails that have been the main fixings for corrugated iron in New Zealand.

elegant shed, Ballinger's house for the Morgans is a milestone. Like many other milestones in the history of New Zealand architecture, it stepped away from the mode of its time, to be accommodated uneasily 20 years later.

That buildings should fit unobtrusively into their context in town or country is part of the conventional wisdom of architecture. It is a moral imperative that can be ignored when works of genius are involved, like the Guggenheim Museum or the Pompidou Centre, but it can be readily invoked to criticise buildings that are unpleasantly prominent or just plain ugly. Queenstown's Lakeland Inn is both prominent and ugly, jammed among the sweet old houses of the lake shore. More than that, it reinforces the impression that Nature's Wonderland is most threatened by the facilities people provide to enjoy it with. In Queenstown, as in other resorts, the eye is assailed by buildings, and the ear by helicopters and jet boats. The Lakeland Inn may be the most offensive building in Queenstown, but the bare suburbs of winter houses there are nearly as crude as summer camp grounds are up north.

The standard gabled units supplied by the Turner brothers of Drummond form a happy family of shapes from which a crib or a house can be assembled. But no amount of green and brown paint can disguise the desperate cliches of the A-frame and the chalet. The wiggly barge boards and Bavarian balcony rails which are deemed to lend an alpine air to the most ordinary holiday house are much less irritating than the pure spiky shapes of steep triangular roof peaks rearing above the road. We are most offended when our attention is demanded by buildings that are inherently banal and unfascinating.

In the open countryside it is hard to disguise buildings except with substantial trees. The old stone houses of Central Otago are usually thought to succeed as compatible additions to the landscape, yet they are really conspicuous, and so are the red tin sheds and the semicircular haybarns that

Sanders house, by John Blair. A spectacular example of the house as object. Blair is unafraid of impressive scenery: he makes houses that stand up strongly against it.

Tennent house, by John Blair.

stand out against the brown and green hills. The painter Rita Angus has seen the sympathy and dissent that recurs in the dialogue between building and land. In her paintings she has marked out the contrasting forms of building and landscape, and then bent the forms and colours of each to bring them together.

John Blair, a Queenstown architect, shows no inclination to make buildings that are hard to see against the great natural scenery in which he often works. Typically, a Blair house is a strongly modelled white sculpture, crisp and clean-edged, uncluttered by appendages or even by borders of greenery.

On the hill above Alexandra are three Blair houses set in a brazen new suburb, and there they are lost. Even on a more open hill face beside the Frankton Arm of Lake Wakatipu, his houses have been rapidly overwhelmed by a tide of new development. But out in the clear countryside they can sing. The Blair house is usually so confidently shaped that it must stand alone against distant hills to be fully appreciated. (Selective photography can achieve a similar effect in reproducing it.)

It is no wonder that the Sanders house, standing on a crest in Dalefield, is known locally as 'the lighthouse'. You can see it and it can see you. It is built like a tree hut, with a stair cranking up the centre; the rooms are platforms around which the exterior skin of the house has been wrapped. The skin is penetrated very selectively to give controlled views of the breathtaking mountain country outside. In this house every window is a picture window.

And the Tennent house, built in 1980, has garages set to one side but linked to the house with a strong roof, leaving an opening at ground level so that the dark mass of the house is penetrated to heighten the view beyond. This house is not unlike one of the Spary's, which Peter Beaven designed to be built near Arrowtown in 1969. The Spary house is a homestead, like the classic farmhouses of Canterbury. Instead of confronting the landscape those houses lie with it, opening into it with doors and verandahs: the farmers who built them did not look at the land, like the tourists of Queenstown, so much as live with it. Don Spary has an almost seamless connection with the whole of Central Otago and Fiordland. He runs a

Spary house, by Peter Beaven. This is a relaxed example of this architect's flair for invention and respect for tradition.

helicopter company, and his own house is a mooring, with a roof of brilliant yellow set beside a tennis court in mown lawn.

That familiarity with the land that farmers feel is not generally expressed in their houses, least of all in those meaty brick bungalows and builders' boxes that dot the Waikato grasslands. They are straying fragments of suburbia, with nothing of the farmhouse about them except a big laundry with a lavatory off it, and a row of gumboots on the back porch.

There are some fine farmhouses in Hawkes Bay, though, and the finest built since the war have been designed by John Scott. In 1967 Scott's Pattison house was built on a gentle brow at Waipawa. The Pattisons had lived in a big square villa, ringed with verandahs – a gracious house, though a good half of it never saw the sun. One night it was burnt to the ground, and nothing remained of it but the family silver, found in a molten blob in the ashes, and now fixed above the fireplace in the new home. The new house sits between the strident object in the landscape and the traditional homestead. It does not look out from under low verandahs in the traditional fashion: instead it is open at the ends, as a whare verandah is an extension of the roof at one end. The roof slips in level at the ridge to form a clerestorey in the manner of the early houses of Group Architects. (John Scott will talk of it as a reminder of the great earthquake, and of the local fault line.)

There is no hint of Colonial mannerism in this building. The main rooms look confidently down the long axis of the house across the kind of cleared domain that homesteads have, tempered by English trees and lawns; and

they look beyond too, into the distant, less cultivated countryside. The house might be seen as New Zealand's arcadian villa. (Connections might be made between the form of this house and the forms favoured by Scott's particular mixture of British and Maori ancestors, but they could only be simple-minded or mischievous.)

OPPOSITE AND THIS PAGE *Pattison house, by John Scott. Scott has a rare sense of the appropriate formal gesture. The Pattison house is a rural villa, beautifully tuned to its owners' needs and detailed with great finesse.*

John Scott has never abandoned the architectural principles he learnt with Group Architects. His buildings are direct, formed of rooms which rely on the intrinsic qualities of their shapes and the materials from which they are crafted. But they are not doggedly functionalist.

The McPhails wanted their house in Havelock North to be essentially made as one room, but the room Scott gave them was not the simplest enclosure for the job. Beneath the embrace of a timbered sheltering roof he side-stepped the walls of the room until he had formed four distinct spaces. He built a kitchen into one corner, 'justified' the extreme height at the roof peak with a tiny mezzanine orator's platform built under it, and bored a circular hole into the high gable end to light the dark roof space. Here he was making up problems to solve, and coming as close as a modernist could to being arbitrary (with the orator's mezzanine) and decorative (with the round window).

On a huge station off the Napier-Taupo road John Scott has built a house for the Apatu family that is locked like a pyramid into the long bleached grass. On this vast, bare site the house is a bastion against the wind and rain and snow. Scott will speak of the form of volcanoes, broken away at one point so the lava flows into the country around. That is the form of this house. Asked again, he will say: 'You take off your saddle, you get your boots off; you want the fire and the warm house around you.' And another day he will talk of the surrounding promontories pricking through the grass swathe like nipples and say that the house picks up those nipple shapes rising out of the rolling plateau.

Since the halcyon Group days of the 1950s, Scott has maintained his own line, as regional architectural styles have developed around Auckland and Christchurch and Wellington. The architectural pacemakers of New Zealand have towed a jet-stream of like souls, opportunists and mimics, behind them. It has been the architect with a distinctive style who drew the fire and the admiration.

Architecture may be intended in the first place to serve practical needs, but it is also a great public art, and the ability to move and excite people with buildings is no less valued now than it has ever been. For the last ten years the very principles that lay behind the work of most architects – the principles of the Modern Movement – have been heavily attacked. Even diehard modernists have shifted the basis of their visual judgement. They find themselves liking now what they disliked intensely ten years ago. Those who once saw modern architecture as the only true road through the battle-ground of the styles now see it too as just another avenue.

BELOW AND NEXT PAGE Apatu house, by John Scott. In overall shape this is a fundamental shelter locked into a plateau of alpine grassland. The building does not stand against the landscape so much as ride with it, echoing the shapes of nearby landforms.

Ngati Poneke Marae, by Rewi Thompson.

6: Risky Horizons

One morning in 1980 an issue of the magazine *Japan Architect* arrived in the Auckland School of Architecture library, advertising an international competition for designs of a 'hometown museum'. The brief did not ask for a 'mausoleum in which things of the past are enshrined in glass cases', but for a 'culture centre and museum for the hometown . . . that will inspire delving into the past, research and growth for the future'. It spoke of how most people's hometowns have 'distinctive histories, traditions, arts and concepts of the neighbourhood', and asked for 'a culture centre and museum that does as the old Oriental saying has it: create the new by learning respect for the old'.

Rewi Thompson looked back to the arrival of his Maori ancestors in New Zealand: '. . . tired and hungry we hauled our canoe high onto the beach. It had carried our people and contained within its hull our culture. We had arrived . . . home.' He modelled a gigantic space frame that rose 200 metres out of Wellington Harbour near the Freyberg Pool and leaned against the hill below Mt Victoria like a beached canoe. Within it, the elements of a marae hung in a glazed lattice of steel in the sparkling Wellington light, honoured and clarified by being thrust into the sky. The formal arrangement began on welcoming platforms at the sea's edge and stretched up through the structure to a lookout at the top. Escalators rose through great frames which

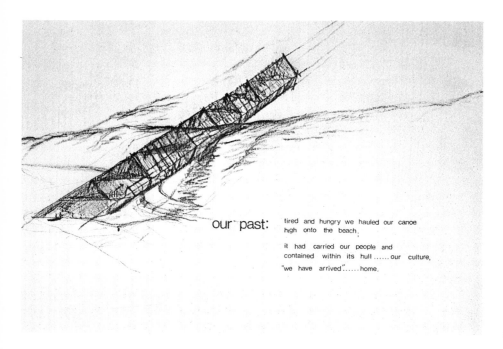

our past: tired and hungry we hauled our canoe high onto the beach.

it had carried our people and contained within its hull ......our culture. "we have arrived".....home.

Ngati Poneke Marae, by Rewi Thompson.

represented the backbone and ribs of the underlying canoe.

In indulging his Maori taste for metaphor, Thompson was also aligning himself knowingly with the post-modern movement that currently dominates world architecture. His grand vision is not a functional answer to a practical problem as most architecture claims to be, but a proposition that demonstrates opportunities, a form that invites its function. Thompson's Ngati Poneke marae project is architecture as a provocative act.

It is a formalist's vision: the main ideas expressed in shape and structure could never be compromised by the impedimenta of functional detail. With a subsequent design in 1984 for a Unesco competition on 'Tomorrow's Habitat' Thompson proposed a house type for a Maori family that elevated a communal sleeping area (the 'kohanga' or nest) above triangular living rooms which opened from the centre of the house, as if to force attention on the outer world. He won the New Zealand section of the competition with an axial, centralized house that matched the monumentality of his marae project. Thompson is one of a coterie of young architects and students from the Auckland School of Architecture who have adopted the grand shapes, the axial geometries, the formal collisions and motifs lifted from architectural history that characterize international post-modernism.

For 35 years the mere sight of buildings shaped in simple geometric forms had been enough to alert and inflame most architects. They believed that architecture must be determined above all by social needs and behaviour patterns, and by a prudent use of physical resources. They were suspicious of buildings that looked as though they had been shaped from the outside: by implication the 'functions' had been stuffed into a jigsaw of rooms squeezed and eased to fit within the external form. Many architects were uneasy in 1956 about the geometries of the new Wanganui War Memorial Hall, and they were as offended by the simple-minded formalism of the Beehive as they were by the knowledge that the government had chosen a rather ordinary British architect, Sir Basil Spence, to design it.

New Zealand architecture, it was thought, had a national stamp. It was mostly made by good keen men who respected the traditions of their country, took on no international airs, and were immune to fashion. The idea that buildings should be designed 'from the inside out', as it used to be put, was of course as naive as the contrary notion that they should be designed from the outside in. And though the good keen men concentrated on the internal organization of their buildings, the best of them learned to keep an eye on the outside as well. They had found out that buildings which truly reflected what went on within them were often inarticulate and unresolved as formal wholes.

It became clear that the exterior could be manipulated by a sensitive architect to evoke emotional reactions and associations which made it coherent in itself. That was one of the lessons taught by Christchurch architects in the 1960s; and if the strengths of Warren and Mahoney might be seen as more formal than spatial, then it is equally true that the quintessential Auckland architects, JASMaD, produce buildings that are often strong internally, but a bit garbled and clumsy in form and vocabulary. (Compare the Auckland University Student Union by Warren and Mahoney to the new Arts/Commerce building there by JASMaD.)

The new formalists are another breed altogether, most concerned with the all-embracing gesture and the appropriate image. So far they do not give a hoot for the development of a national style, though the tasks they set themselves are sometimes particularly local – as we have seen in Thompson's marae and kohanga, and will later notice in Bossley's d'Urville Island dwelling, and Lane's museum in Helensville.

Thompson's architecture for Maori families and communities probably has no more chance of national acceptance than Group Architects' plans for middle-class families had in 1950. There is a comfortable elitism about the new formalists which is easy to accept in architecture that remains as sketches and plans and is never built. On the other hand, the unprecedented publicity of the last ten years for projects and competition entries that are never intended to be built tempts architects to make spectacular but hollow gestures that demand attention as formal and graphic summaries, but are neither complex nor subtle as architectural realities.

In 1984 even the mainstream architectural world here sees the catch-cries of the 1940s, 50s and 60s as Utopian and puritanical. Middle-of-the-road architects no longer reject decoration or think a building has to show how and why it is built as it is. 'Modern architecture' has turned into a term to describe buildings that were based on those ideas of directness and honesty. The modern cliche was the international office building, and the cliche of modernist criticism is condemnation of it. Too often the face of modernism was like the commercial backside of office blocks that line The Terrace in Wellington. Yet the same architectural language was used to rebuild Wellington below The Terrace during the 1970s, and from down on the Quay it reads as a great commercial vernacular – full of individual gaucheries, to be sure, but as exciting en masse as the earlier vernacular of Victorian housing stepping up the hillsides around the town.

In this country, modernism was under serious threat from the day Ian Athfield turned the first sod on his Khandallah section and started to build his free-form, afunctional house and workplace. Even architects had become embarrassed by their recent past. They were being lambasted by those vogue professionals the sociologists and town planners, and journalists too were striking out against the big systematic grids that covered city buildings. Architects had tried to handle large numbers of people with simple gestures, categorizing problems and repeating solutions. The modern approach was as clear in the instant town of Twizel as in any city centre.

By the late 1960s some architects were being caught up in the Whole Earth movement. They looked towards a new Utopia based on small communities. The vision was backward-looking, and so in the main was its architecture, but it attacked the corporate image of business. It rejected the grid, the cube, the office block and most things 'straight'. And it celebrated the personal, the individual, the eccentric.

The hippie flavour flashed in the architectural bloodstream like a rogue hormone. For the first time in this century architects felt they could look back, plundering history and the architecture of other cultures. Peter

ABOVE AND OPPOSITE University of Auckland Music School, by Manning and Mitchell. Even the most demanding physical functions deserve a response that is poetic as well as practical.

Beaven's little Italianate office building for the Canterbury Building Society in Auckland was the first city building to be shamelessly referential. The moral weight of modernism had bored Beaven before most people had questioned it.

Historicism of a sort had always been popular in the suburbs of course. Budding home-owners could look back across the whole of architectural history in search of a style with which to be identified, limited only by capital and confidence. After 30 years of trying to drag an unwilling public round to the idea that unadorned functionalism was what they needed, architects at last began to yield to the public view. They dallied. They could never align themselves with the vulgar tastes of the common throng, but they could pluck from the noble vocabulary of the Renaissance, or from the peasantry of some country not their own.

Architects are prepared to admit now that making buildings which function, in the crude sense, is one of the simpler tasks in architecture. They are looking for new sources, asking where architectural images come from, playing with the language of buildings.

When Jack Manning and I were designing the Music School building at Auckland University in 1980 we knew there was no logical connection between the side of a grand piano and the shape of a noise-reflecting street wall, but artistically it seemed perfectly reasonable for one to mirror the other. Before we had even been sent the brief for the building we had discussed the possibility of a masking wall cut between the relics of two old buildings on the site, concealing a courtyard. The baroque style of the plan probably appeared as an analogue of the freedoms music suggests. Such preoccupations precede the physical analysis of requirements, and they are then shaped to answer the demands of the brief.

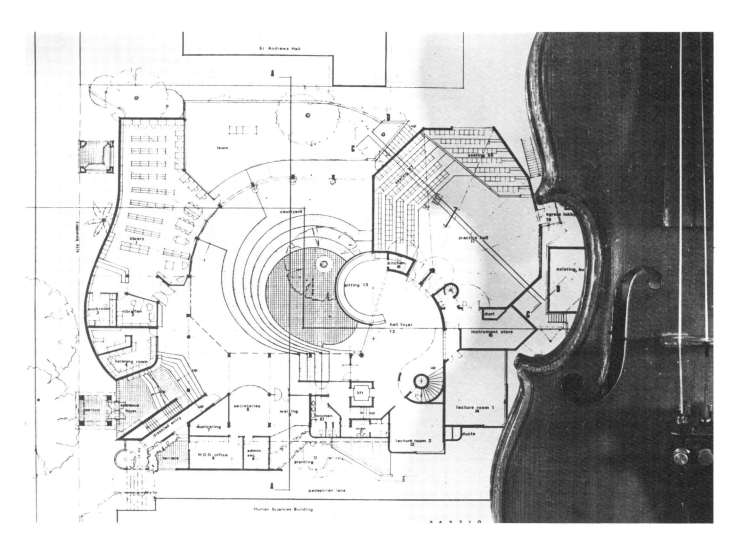

St Andrews Hall

lawn

courtyard

library

sitting 13

hall foyer
13

workroom
3   librarian

listening room

practice hall

kitchen

existing bu

duct

instrument store

lecture room 1

portico

foyer

disabled entry

secretaries

waiting

lift

up

women

men

up

lecture room 2

terrace

duplicating

H.O.D. office

admin
sec

planting

ducts

site boundary

pedestrian lane

Human Sciences Building

OVERLEAF, LEFT AND TOP RIGHT First *Church of Christ Scientist, by Athfield Architects. The sources of architecture may be explicable, without being entirely rationally related to the buildings they inspire.*

OVERLEAF, BOTTOM RIGHT Napier Street *Townhouses, Auckland, by Cook Hitchcock and Sargisson. These 'gelato' houses are as stylish as any townhouses being built in the country, though their impact diminishes a little as their numbers multiply.*

So the street wall is turned in the architects' minds from glass to concrete as its noise-controlling role is understood, and it is curved and textured to give it a charm it might not have needed had it been made of glass. Once the generator of baroque form has been thus laid down, the manner of the whole plan is set, to be embellished by the ingenious solution of physical problems.

The courtyard is gently tiered to take an outdoor audience; balconies appear around it controlling the noise between rooms while gracing them with an extension to the outdoors. Manipulating the complex acoustics becomes just part of shaping the building as a social setting. The building is not principally the product of its formal brief.

It is hard to admit, but one might find the basis of a building in the shape of a piece of chewing gum on the sole of one's shoe. To be such an opportunist about the origins of form is not to deny a place for architectural craftsmanship: it is to assert that fine architecture is not merely a kind of inspired practicality. Ideas linger in the imagination waiting for an excuse to be used, looking for a place to fit.

Ian Athfield's church for the Christian Scientists, built in Wellington in 1983, could hardly have sprung simply from a rational analysis of his task. The Church discouraged their architect from using any of the symbols of Christianity common to architecture. Lectures, not sermons, were to be offered in the main room. Questions were to be asked by the very architecture of the building. Athfield agrees that he has used architectural

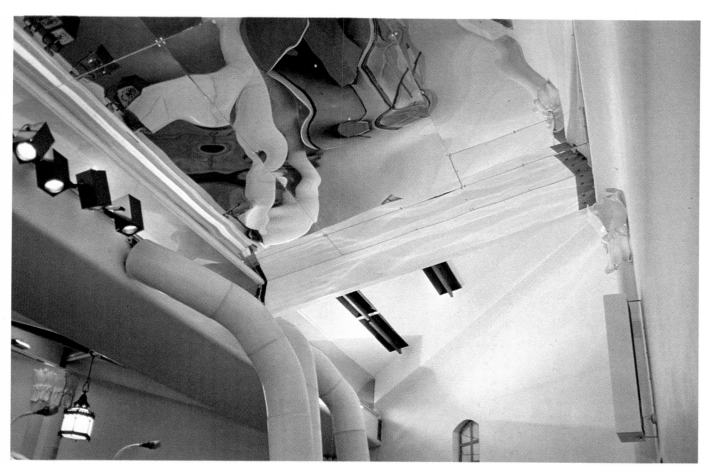

symbols to stand in for religious ones, but he is understandably cagey about attributing specific meanings to them. Others have jumped in with their own interpretations. Tommy Honey sees the high stained glass window above the entry as a baleful eye in an empty skull, and the 'uncompleted' columns of the interior as a symbol of decay. Others see more cheerful things: to some the bent and straight columns trimmed with pink ceramic capitals resemble a woman's legs with a petticoat showing below a white skirt. To most observers the stairway up the roof can only lead to heaven, though the nature of heaven is an open subject that is presumably discussed downstairs.

This building is full of transposed references: there are Tudor church doors under a stainless steel and glass reinterpretation of the Colonial verandah, a lolloping, soft white roof that is domed like a head, with a stained-glass eye looking out from what turns out inside to be an unoccupied mezzanine platform housing the pneumatic equipment of the organ. The lectern and the seating behind it are styled a little like an FJ Holden, while many of the windows have cute shutters with Colonial louvres.

It might seem unsporting in a time when 'multi-valent meanings', historical references, masks and jokes are the substance of architectural fashion, to question whether there is an inner logic to this building; or if there is, to ask whether the building might not have lost its central voice in a clamour of architectural noise. The inconsistencies that it wears on its sleeve certainly prompt passers-by to ask questions – and that seems to be what the Church members had called for. Athfield may deliberately have left the building unresolved. That is a post-modern fascination. It shows in the Auckland Music School building, and it is part of a current interest in making architecture that is not what it appears to be. But the reason for the disjunctions of the Church of Christ Scientist may be more simple than that: more than most architects, Athfield allows the sublime innocence of the imagination to appear, uncensored, in his finished buildings. It is perhaps his greatest strength.

The Auckland architects Cook Hitchock and Sargisson are artful by comparison. They currently work in a house style that is neo-Arts and Crafts. Their recently built townhouses have relatively standard internal arrangements, with veneered external 'wallpapers' of stucco in pastel hues, relieved with cottage windows and occasional shutters. Marshall Cook, once an apprentice of Group Architects, has identified the need for stylistic variety: 'Group Architects only had one style and they built the same way whether in Titirangi or Takapuna. We want to build in character with the suburb.'

Cook's horses-for-courses approach has so far barely been tested outside the inner suburbs, but there are subtle distinctions in style between his Napier Street terrace houses in Freemans Bay – camp, cut-rate comfort, with sunny courts and a townsy air – and his more indulgent Remuera block, – 'The Close'. This group of houses on a rear lot has composed windows that for a moment seem Georgian, temple-like entrances that are saved from pretension by architectural humour, and hefty pergolas with the beam-ends shaped. The architect directs attention at the elements of the house which traditionally indicate status. He draws the exterior view of each wall with painstaking care, as if it has a life as an image that is independent of the complex behaviour of the people behind it. The plan is open, quite free, unremarkable. The wilful exterior patternmaking that Miles Warren was once accused of by Bill Wilson is here developed to an extreme degree by one of Wilson's own old pupils. 'Wallpaper?' says Cook. 'Yes, but very sophisticated wallpaper!'

The wallpaper on the outside of the Murphy house by Mal Bartleet is heavily embossed. This 1983 house of cards in Grey Lynn is relatively unsurprising internally, but most people who see it from the street are stopped in their tracks. It is a simple Fibro box on stilts, transformed on the

Skyscraper proposed by Mies van der Rohe, 1919. Auckland University Architecture Library.

outside by a layer of diagonal timber trellis fixed over the Fibro and in places over the windows too. Here and there, classical emblems of architecture emerge from the latticed walls and stick out from the entrance portico or the bay window. This is shameless robbery from the archives of world architectural history. It would be impossible to guess from inside that the house looked remotely as it does from the street. The idea of congruence between inside and out has been staunchly promoted since 1920, but it was not an issue of concern in many previous periods of architecture. The Murphy house is the most striking example in New Zealand of the entertaining deceptions that can be woven by a skilled player of decorative games.

But is that architecture? Certainly the study of style and mannerism has dominated several other periods of architecture. Close to our own time are the styles of Art Deco and Art Nouveau, and there are many examples in public building of the eclectic styles of the Beaux Arts – academic pieces from the pre-modern era. These are more and more loudly heralded now that the brave new world modern architecture tried to make is found wanting. Still, there is a lingering suspicion that beguiling decoration indicates a lack of something beneath. The new eclecticism may express nothing more than a simple yearning for more comfortable times, or it may represent an elite conservatism – a kind of Ponsonby Chic. Architects might

Napier Street Townhouses.

be moving closer to a larger public by embracing the historicist and pictorial aspects of architecture we have seen in the hometown, or they may be setting up stylistic havens for the cognoscenti. History shows that exclusiveness has been the initial strength and the ultimate weakness of many an architectural style.

Some of the most interesting architectural ideas never get built but have a life of their own as drawings: Mies van der Rohe's evocative drawings of glass skyscrapers in 1919 altered the course of architecture around the

Murphy house, by Mal Bartleet. The most thorough and extreme example of applied decoration in post-war professional architecture in New Zealand.

D'Urville Island house, by Peter Bossley.

world. That may be too much to ask of Pete Bossley's drawings for the entrance to a botanic garden in South Auckland submitted in a design competition in 1979. They formed too fond and amusing a comment on suburban gardening to be taken seriously by judges looking for dignity before affection. Bossley proposed to build as a momument a towering garden fork that was thrust into the ground at the street frontage of the garden. You simply drove in between the left-hand prongs and out between the right-hand ones. Here was art, commerce and local authority aggrandizement brought together in a single offering. But it looked as though he was taking the mickey out of all three. Commentary of this sort cuts no ice with the captains of local government here. The arch of greenery with which Archangels won the competition was more gentle and pleasing, but it lacked the resonances of Bossley's proposal.

In the Auckland School of Architecture Library one picture is enlarged

A.R.A.
BOTANIC GARDEN
ENTRANCE   PETE BOSSLEY & ALLIED ST.

Entrance gate to Manukau City Botanic Garden, by Peter Bossley. No entry in this competition was more appropriate than this monument to the suburban garden. Bossley uses the techniques of commercial advertizing with zest and fun.

beyond all others. It shows a man sitting on the verandah of a hut surrounded by flax and scrub – the precursor of the Auckland architect's house of the 1940s. There on the verandah is the 'man alone' of New Zealand literature. This simple building might even be Adam's house in Paradise. But man alone has outstayed his welcome. He has accepted company and given up fighting in a few seductive sketches Bossley has made of a dream house for a couple on a d'Urville Island beach. These could be the illustrations of a bedtime book for adults. Functionally, they mark out a shelter from the storm. But there is no brief, and there are no clients – Bossley is speculating, conjuring up a formal vision of the unencumbered life. His ideal couple might make expeditions in the boat they keep in the basement, or they might make sorties along the beach, but it is hard to avoid the conclusion that their task in life is to make love while surf hisses on the sand below. Their house is a bastion against the forces of the everyday world.

That is a role the bach once took in the poetic imagination. The beach house has almost replaced it, but the myth of the bach still lives, and holiday

'Man alone' could never be better represented than in this anonymous photograph that is held like a banner for truth in the Auckland University School of Architecture. Auckland University Architecture Library.

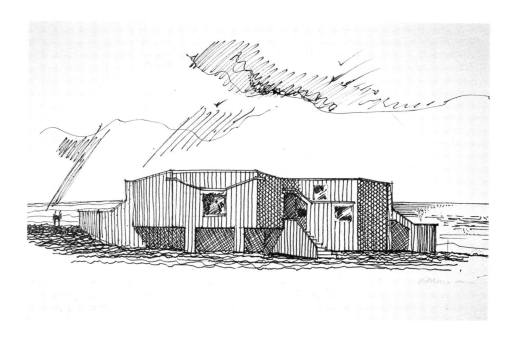

Begg Beach house proposal, Opito, by David Mitchell.

houses are still testing grounds for ideas that later find their way into the home. The Begg house at Opito that I designed in 1979 was an early example here of the front wall used deliberately to mask the building behind. Any bach on the dunes must face in two directions. Here, an enigmatic wall of lies faces the road, and the bach lounges against the back of it looking out to sea.

Nigel Cook has suggested a way of bringing home the summer life at the bach: he starts with the idea that our task is to make habitable the natural paradise we have. Couldn't we live in the garden, he asks, if only we had shelter from the rain? That might be difficult in Invercargill, but on the Hauraki Gulf and in Northland it should not be too hard to arrange. In his Waiheke house Cook set rooms like islands in the bush, with a glass and latticed roof between them to trap and control a slice of the natural landscape. It is as if the house were made of separate buildings, with just enough cover to stop you getting wet on the way to bed. The kitchen is a nucleus which served the garden as well as a more enclosed dining place.

Though architects have ideas waiting to be used when the chance arises,

Palace/Cook house, Waiheke Island, by Nigel Cook. Sooner or later Nigel Cook or someone else will build the house that makes a seamless connection with the landscape. Cook has been working on this vision for five or ten years.

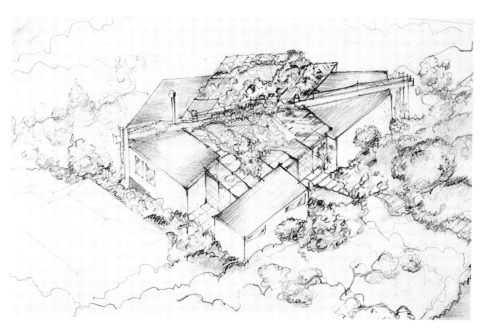

Gibbs house, by David Mitchell. This house makes no reference to the dominant post-war Auckland style. It has more to do with international modernism and with the plastered Moderne houses of Auckland's harbour slopes.

most buildings are also shaped by the people who will occupy them or, in the commercial arena, by the people who will pay for them. One can discuss architectural ideas without reference at all to the clients of architects: ideas have a life of their own. But fortunately clients have a great influence on architecture too – not merely in attending to the practicalities that, legend has it, architects ignore, but in setting the style and calling the tune.

The 1984 Gibbs house is a big pavilion that I designed for lovers of cool and modern architecture. Clients who do not want natural timber to show in their house are extremely rare in this country: the Gibbs wanted none of it.

Their house has some of its roots in the International Style. If the Utopian politics of modernism cannot be seen here, the Utopian aesthetics can. We have learnt that kit of parts, and we can read it fluently. In the Gibbs house it is occasionally upset by a geometric overlay askew to the rectilinear framework. A big angled wall reaches out from the house towards the harbour heads, and an outsize steel frame that is hardly just functional steps from the living room into the garden. But for all its otherworldly grandeur, it

ABOVE
Gibbs house, David Mitchell.

is an Auckland house. The huge silver roof, the clean-cornered patio falling sheer into the swimming pool, the white roughcast walls and the elaborate mirrored bathrooms are all updates on the elements of the great white houses of the Orakei and St Heliers cliffs. This 'other' architecture of Auckland was still being made when Group Architects first launched themselves, but it has been largely ignored as a local bloodline.

The Auckland Style that started with Vernon Brown has mellowed in the hands of a few architects, and the tub-thumping rhetoric of the 1940s has faded. Nick Stanish and Briar Green have designed a simple subtle house

Evans house, by Nick Stanish and Briar Green. The humanist tradition that was set in Auckland in the 1940s is sensitively recalled and gently embellished here.

that arcs about a Titirangi garden. The Evans house built in 1983 is virtually one space subdivided by screens and a change in level that lifts the bedroom above the living area. Stanish shapes his buildings strongly around social groups, reflecting his own sense of family unity and elevating domestic ritual. He focuses attention on specific social activity – eating a meal, sitting in front of the fire, cooking and talking. He is not averse to arranging the main spaces of a house around an axis that strengthens their importance by formalizing their layout. Stanish has no truck with fashion, which makes his buildings seem unusually direct.

One might expect Roger Walker's tin shed for a plumber to be direct too. But Walker is a compulsive complicator who has been heard to say that because corrugated iron can be curved he will not have it any other way. His Gas House in Gisborne, built in 1982, is a real shed, a funny shed, a piece of plumbing for a plumber. The buildings around it are the kind that formed the opening subject in this book. Unlike them, Gas House is a three-dimensional piece of architecture, not just a box with a sign on it. The building is its own sign. Ironically, one of the few structures we have looked at that functions as a shed is really a piece of high design; its architectural features are intrinsic in the best modern manner. It has none of the crummy old tricks of the folk builders. They are now found instead in cultivated architecture of the noblest purpose – in false-fronted flats, in buildings of all kinds styled neo-Classical, neo-Georgian, and even neo-Modern.

But no architect can be innocent in the way the folk builder can, secure in knowing that there is never anything wrong with making one's own world. Architects must continually adjust to other people's patterns of life, and that is the least problem they face. Right now many feel as if the entire basis of their beliefs and performance has been cut away by brilliant academic denunciations of the principles that modern architects had proudly clung to as fundamental verities for 60 years. Now, in the heady flush of late- and post-modern experimentation, architects can do what they like. But they are not sure where to move.

Allen Curnow's *Landfall in Unknown Seas* states the plight:

> But now there are no more islands to be found
> And the eye scans risky horizons of its own
> In unsettled weather, and murmurs of the drowned
>   Haunt their familiar beaches –
> Who navigates us towards what unknown
>
> But not improbable provinces? Who reaches
> A future down for us from the high shelf
> Of spiritual daring? Not those speeches
>   Pinning on the Past like a decoration
> For merit that congratulates itself . . .

It would be easy for architects merely to cultivate a new eclectism, and we might not object to that if we got an architecture which approached the rich body of revivalist building the Victorians gave us. But that is unlikely: today too many colours stain the general tide for a pattern of shades to emerge.

Some of the best architects are enriching architecture with references to language and history and context. There is a critical reaction against the faddishness and superficiality of much post-modern building around the world, though the minor talents of architecture can hardly be blamed for picking up the visual mannerisms of the best. So far, within the several streams of contemporary architecture here, only Imi Porsolt has spoken for a new architectural austerity to match the economic austerity of our time. Nostalgia and sentimentality seem to flourish best in the leanest years, and the rationality of modernism is too close to be acceptable. Finally, no one has yet made winning images of a new austerity.

Evans house, by Stanish and Green.

Gas house, Gisborne, by Roger Walker. The outsize details and the rolling tin and glass turn this shed into an entertaining industrial cartoon.

THIS IS HELENSVILLE, MY TINY
NEW ZEALAND HOMETOWN, BETWEEN
THE MEANDERING RIVER & PASSING
ROAD I BUILD A GRANITE SLAB
OVER THE RUBBISH TIP, AN
ENTRANCE PORTICO, A MIRROR
WALL AND AN OBELISK.
THEY MAP & MARK THE TOWN
WHILE IT RISES AND FALLS WITH
PASSING TIME.
TEMPORARY GRANDEUR.

*Hometown Museum made of the
Helensville Rubbish Tip by Noel Lane.
This project has a powerful formal sense
that is rare in New Zealand architecture,
though it can also be seen in Rewi
Thompson's Ngati Poneke Marae
building.* Photographer Denise Moore.

The biggest and best architectural ideas never need an obvious pedigree.
They are as unlikely and as undeniable as thunder. Noel Lane comes from
the kind of town that I discussed in the first chapter. Like Rewi Thompson,
Lane designed a museum for his hometown and won a prize in the Japanese
competition from which the brief had come. His extraordinary proposal did
not even have a building in it: Lane had monumentalized the Helensville
rubbish tip. As a child he had fossicked there for treasure, and his
competition entry was essentially three coloured photographs of a model of
the town dump – the resting place, to him, of Helensville's culture. There he
had walled in a rectangle like a suburban plot, isolating a patch of the tip
through which the tidal river runs, and marked its axis with the town by an
obelisk. A polished black slab of granite floated above the rubbish as a
tipping platform for trucks which entered the site through a portico and
mirror-wall designed to reflect the enduring hills about the town. As
Helensville rose and fell through centuries, relics of Lane's project were to
remain like archaeological signals – slab, portico, perimeter wall, obelisk –
each as monumental in its context as the subjects in surrealist paintings.

Late one night Denise Moore photographed Lane's model as he
compressed the passage of a thousand future years, building houses and
gardens around the grandest dump in the world, setting them on fire,
smashing the mirror, sweeping the scene with sand.

Lane's images were as primal as a drum beat, able to be felt by anyone
regardless of how fully they were understood. Like Thompson's marae
project, Lane's rubbish dump was a heroic piece of public art. Both
proposals possessed a monumental grandeur that had always been missing
in New Zealand architecture. And what they monumentalized were the
processes of everyday life in this country.

Index

Love it or hate it, the architectural face of New Zealand that most of us know best has a skin of weatherboard, brick veneer and glass. It is the face of the bungalow, the school and the dairy, the kindergarten down the road and the pub on the corner. Most of the buildings we live among are such stock items that merely mentioning their names conjures up a precise image in the mind's eye.

Not many post-war architects have been fossicking for the mother-lode of folk architecture here – they've been busy making their own myths. The idea of the elegant shed was one: it caught hold of the architectural imagination in the mid forties, when Vernon Brown's black and white lean-to houses began popping up on Auckland's northern slopes. Led by Group Architects, the Auckland architects of the fifties were carried along by post-war optimism, broadly socialist ideals and a belief in the homegrown Kiwi way of doing things. They were modernists to the heart.

By contrast, the urbane manners of Christchurch architects Miles Warren and Peter Beaven, and Ted McCoy in Dunedin, grew out of their respect for the nineteenth century traditions of their own cities. They leaned towards contemporary English models; it was Warren who elevated the cottage and made the first convincing townhouses in New Zealand since the thirties.

By the seventies, the most striking innovators were building on the Wellington hills. Roger Walker and Ian Athfield invented fractured, irrational, impassioned buildings that were modernist heresies. And the rebellion against modernism has gathered force in the eighties. These days only the old-hats continue the revolutionary spirit of modern architecture. Today's radicals look backwards for their sources – to Victorian New Zealand, Renaissance Italy, classical Greece and even ancient Egypt.

This book has grown out of a television series called 'The Elegant Shed', which was a survey of the last forty years of New Zealand architecture. David Mitchell, who wrote and presented the series, is a well known architect, who also lectures on architecture at the University of Auckland. Gillian Chaplin is a photographer whose work has been widely exhibited. She was co-author of Mihaia, published by OUP in 1979.

Front cover: Gibbs House, by David Mitchell
Back cover: Farm shed, Hawkes Bay

Oxford University Press
ISBN 0 19 558125 3